the Secret Olympian

by Anon

THE INSIDE STORY OF THE OLYMPIC EXPERIENCE

BLOOMSBURY

LONDON · BERLIN · NEW YORK · SYDNEY

For S with love

Published in the UK in 2012 by Bloomsbury Publishing Plc
50 Bedford Square, London WC1B 3DP
www.bloomsbury.com

ISBN 978 1 4081 5492 2

3 5 7 9 10 8 6 4 2

A CIP catalogue record for this book is available from the British Library.

This book is produced using paper that is made from wood grown in
managed, sustainable forests. It is natural, renewable and recyclable. The
logging and manufacturing processes conform to the environmental
regulations of the country of origin.

Typeset in Perpetua by seagulls.net

Printed and bound in England by Clays Ltd, St Ives plc

the Secret
Olympian

It's not the winning but the struggle.

Le Baron de Coubertin

CONTENTS

In this book I hope to give you an insight into what it is actually like to experience an Olympic Games as an athlete – of what really goes on. Not just what it's like to a win a gold medal but also what it's like to be an Olympian. The excitement and expectation after being anointed as one of the chosen few. The inevitable mind-bending pressure before the performance of your life. Then the extreme psychological release after competition and the mind-blowing parties as the fittest people in the world celebrate or commiserate their life-defining moments. Finally, the ultimate come-down afterwards as you return to Earth and become mortal once again.

I was in Athens as part of Team GB, at the Greeks' lastminute.com Games in August 2004. I watched the flames lick from the Olympic torch at one end of the stadium, like a giant plastic fire-lighter. The smell of fresh paint floated everywhere. Many of the sporting venues, roads, trams and railways were finished in late July/early August, just days before the Games began. It cost Greece €9 billion. Sounds a bit silly now, with the country on the verge of bankruptcy, but at the time their Games were seen as a great success. No gold medals for me, sadly, but 'been there and got the T-shirt' and the other 35kg of official Team GB kit.

Being an Olympian changes you. For some, the changes are immense and last the rest of their days. Get a lucky (or even a well-deserved) break and, depending on your profile and what else is on TV when your conpetition airs, you can be financially secure with a career in broadcasting or public speaking stretching ahead of you. For others, the changes are smaller. They return with good memories, great stories and incriminating photos, and quietly reinsert themselves into everyday life. But their view of themselves is forever slightly altered, having been amongst the best in the world at something. You can go to the Games for those three magical weeks and come back a hero. Or you can come back an asshole. Sometimes both. Or you never quite come back at all, forever regretting some small failure or slip which no one else remembers.

Mine is only one perspective of the Olympic experience so I persuaded many other Olympians of various nationalities, ages and sports to let me interview them, often under condition of anonymity, and to ask questions like – what's life like inside the Olympic Village? How do you cope with the once-in-a-lifetime pressure and tomorrow being the biggest day of your life? Which teams hold the best parties? Is there as much sex as everyone makes out? And, having achieved your life's goal in your early 20s, where the hell do you go from there?

the realisation

You're going to the Olympics

Oxfordshire, UK
1 July 2004

I'm shocked to see the head coach smiling and, more specifically, smiling at me outside the training centre, as I work on some of our racing gear. Doesn't happen often. Takes me back to the World Championships' medal podium 11 months ago, the last time the leathery, out-all-day-for-30-years-in-all-weathers face creased into a smile beneath the trademark sunglasses.

My head coach is the best in the world at what he does, which is coaching, training and selecting athletes. His charges have won gold medals at every Olympics for decades now. In my sport he is God.

And God is smiling upon me.

'Congratulations,' he says in a voice almost as leathery as his face, the thick gravelly accent remaining despite almost two decades in the UK. He extends a hand over the top of my racing equipment. I start shaking it, not quite believing what I suddenly realise is about to happen. 'You're going to the Olympics.'

The magic words every athlete wants to hear. The Olympics. Only for the best of the best of the best. Watched by billions. The athletes' Everest. The maker of legends.

Pretty cool for a Thursday morning.

And I'm doubly surprised. Two weeks ago we'd had the opposite conversation. God had looked stern, a more natural set of his features. 'Ya, OK, so now we take the next step.' And the next step was the World Championships for non-Olympic events, held alongside the Junior World Championships, a sort of special circle of hell for the Olympic also-rans. The senior athletes looking and feeling vaguely inappropriate, like they're hanging around a school's back gate.

But now there's been a team re-shuffle. I'm going to the Olympics.

Just one downside. I'm going to have to eBay the consolation two week holiday to Sri Lanka.

Girlfriend won't be happy.

Take a breath

Ask an Olympian about the how they felt the moment they knew they were going to the Olympics and from most you get a surprisingly subdued and downbeat answer. You might imagine it would be all leaping up and down, arms raised to the heavens, then tears of happiness and heartfelt embraces with nearest and dearest. But no. One Beijing medallist I asked about how he felt at that moment replied, 'It was so unimportant that I don't remember.'

Another Beijing medallist and Athens veteran relived the moment he discovered he was going to the Olympics for the first time. 'Oh, yeah, I remember. We were all really pissed off because it had been so badly handled. It still hacks me off today. We read about our selection in a press release. It was pathetic.'

The truth is that most see selection or rejection coming; my own case was unusual. After months and months of selection and trials, and often several years of World Championships results, the athletes generally know who's in and who's out well before the coaches sit them down. By the time you open the letter or go into the meeting with the head coach you know what's coming, so it's a bit of a non-event.

In sprint cycling for example, the reigning World Champion and World Cup winners in disciplines like the keirin and sprint are automatically provided a slot at the Olympics. Athletics is similar; British athletes qualify based on performances at the British trials and by reaching qualifying times set by the International Association of Athletics Federation.

Nick Bell fenced the individual and team foil at two Olympics. 'You know from the season's results and the ranking system. You're not on tenterhooks. In all the times I went [to the Olympics] I knew I would go long before the selector's phone call.'

Josh West, the 6'10" giant who rowed in the British eight in Athens and Beijing, echoes Nick. 'It's a moment along the way which you recognise but it doesn't feel like an achievement. There's such a long build up to the whole thing, but it's mostly relief and a sense of, that's done, now the next step.'

Like Josh, most Olympians I spoke to agreed that the final confirmation comes as a relief; a relief that the sacrifices and striving have been recognised, rather than as a cause for euphoric celebration. Indeed, since Team GB's disastrous Olympics in Atlanta 1996 (one solitary gold), a number of athletes think the British Olympic Association (BOA) has intentionally made the final selection of the team for the Olympics less of 'an event', less of an end in itself, trying to stamp out a culture noted by some of the top British performers in Atlanta of 'getting the jersey as the goal.' As one Beijing medallist told me, 'There was a lot of deliberate effort [by the BOA] post '96 to make "getting a result at the Olympics" the goal. Getting the jersey was just what you had to do to in order to get the result.'

Perhaps the previous focus on 'the jersey' was understandable. Many athletes were amateurs up against full-time professionals. Today though, with National Lottery funding, British Olympians can compete on a level playing field. They can and do have a different attitude, and it shows in their results. Today's Olympians might allow themselves one night to revel in the realisation and satisfaction after the announcement, often having a celebratory dinner with parents and loved ones, but then they return to training and business as usual the next morning.

The other reason for a lack of euphoria on final selection is that selection is never that final. An injury or a loss of form and you'll be dropped. Some coaches like to keep their athletes guessing about selection until the last minute, a much-resented attempt to prevent complacency and squeeze the best from them. One Beijing Olympian reported, 'The coach always wants to be a step ahead so he's very reluctant to communicate. He never gets cornered easily. It was made clear that any slip and you'd be dropped anyway.' All athletes recognise that you're never safe until you're on the starting blocks. What they resent is the coaches constantly reminding them of that and the culture of fear that creates.

Emotions can run much higher on the day of selection in ball sports like hockey or football, where picking a team is more subjective. The day of reckoning can be brutal. Steve Batchelor, who won 48 England hockey caps and played at three Olympics, notably on the wing of Britain's gold medal team in Seoul '88 (a feat which subsequent teams have shown no hint of equalling), remembers, 'When we got picked they used to sit the 24 members of the squad on the grass outside Bisham Abbey. Then they'd read out the 16 who were going.' Dreams shattered or lifetime goals achieved in an instant. 'It was quite tough,' says Steve with masterly understatement. Steve was always on the right side of the call; others weren't so fortunate.

'We [the squad] were up in Sophia Gardens in Cardiff for our final training session before the Barcelona team got picked. I was rooming with one of the new boys to the squad. I got picked. He didn't. We had to go back and pack our bags up and he had an absolute go at me, "You shouldn't be going," and all this. I just said sorry. I mean, what do you say? I don't know why they put us in a room together. It was so awkward. But he got to play in two Olympics after that so [in retrospect] it wasn't the end of the world.' Today, with the benefit of much water under the bridge, Steve is really good friends with his old squad mate. And these days the hockey selectors write letters.

Whilst most athletes see Olympic selection coming from a distance, just occasionally unforeseen events intervene with far-reaching consequences, as Batchelor recalls:

'In 1983 we ranked 13th in the world in hockey. Which is nothing. Twelve teams go to the Olympics, so we weren't going. So I went off and played the tennis circuit.' One of those annoyingly multi-talented people, Batchelor played junior international tennis alongside Jeremy Bates and Andrew Castle and toured the pro tennis circuit when hockey allowed.

Then, in May 1984, while playing a tournament in the south of France, Batchelor was surprised by a call from the GB hockey coach, Roger Self. 'Come back to training camp. The Russians have pulled out.'

Citing the commercialisation of the Olympics and 'anti-Soviet prop-aganda', the USSR pulled out of the 1984 LA Games 12 weeks before the opening ceremony. A wave of boycotts from more than a dozen Communist-leaning allies followed. It was a clear middle finger to the US in retribution for the American-led boycott of the Moscow 1980 Games, where more than 60 countries pulled athletes after the Russian invasion of Afghanistan. The British hockey team was one of the few beneficiaries of the Cold War and was promoted into the magic dozen.

'So,' smiles Batchelor, clearly enjoying the flashback sitting in the sunshine of his garden, not far from the Steve Batchelor Hockey and Tennis Academy, 'I came back, got in the squad and off we went. And we got a bronze medal. Now that's what I call luck.' They beat the Australians 3–2 to the medal.

But the Cold War really paid off for the team several years later. Buoyed by their surprise success and having had a 'fantastic time amongst all the superstars' in Los Angeles, the team largely kept playing elite level hockey whilst managing day jobs as tennis coaches, surgeons, policemen or school teachers. LA success also brought in some spon-sorship. No longer would the team have to pay for their national team tracksuits. They went on to silver in the 1986 World Cup in London, behind their old adversaries the Australians. Ten of the 1984 bronze medallists went to Seoul in 1988. 'If '84 hadn't happened it would have been a very, very different team,' says Batchelor.

They went on to win the gold medal, beating the Australians 3–2 again in the semi-final. Without the Russian invasion of Afghanistan, it would have been a very different story: a happier Australian hockey team, no gold medal for Britain and no Steve Batchelor Academy.

The Olympic dream fallacy

One of the first trials of the recently christened Olympian-to-be is the local newspaper interview. The journalist is buzzing, looking forward to an uplifting story of the local boy or girl made good.

The obligatory first question, 'How long have you dreamed of being an Olympian?'

The automatic response, 'Since I was a kid' or 'Since I can remember.'

Whilst such a response may make a nice sound bite and an uplifting 'Dream comes true for local boy' page two lead, in the main it's not actually true. I didn't dream about going to the Olympics and neither did most of my compatriots. We answer yes to the leading question from journalists because it seems expected and it sounds ungrateful not to have dreamt of going.

Most Olympians did watch the Games avidly as kids and had sporting heroes whom they idolised, but most never seriously thought it might one day be them. And their idols generally weren't in the sports they ended up succeeding in.

Hockey gold medallist Batchelor idolised tennis player Ilie Nastase, the temperamental Romanian lothario. 'I loved him to death. I had a bit of a temper like him. I just thought he was the best ever.'

West, the rowing giant, thought the winter Olympics way cooler. 'I'd go skiing on the weekends and watch racing afterwards. Alberto Tomba was my hero.' Why the change from downhill skiing? 'Have you looked at me?' At 6'10", Josh would cut quite a dash in a full body, lime green, ski Lycra. A number of British Olympians (non-track and field) obsessed with the Steve Ovett and Seb Coe rivalry of the late 1970s and early 1980s, some watching Moscow transfixed when barely out of kindergarten. Others are less traditional. British Beijing gold medallist

Tom James didn't have a sporting idol. He preferred Jimmy Hendrix: 'He re-wrote the rules.'

Tom didn't give any thought as a kid to being an Olympian one day, in fact he struggled to believe he was at the Olympics even on the day he became Olympic Champion. 'You feel so separate from what you think an Olympic champion should be that even at the point you are sitting on the start of the Olympic final you still don't feel like this is right, like this is how it should be. You almost imagine, when you see it on TV, that's there's something special about it, that they know something you don't. Afterwards you know it's exactly the same concept as what you were doing when you were 13, just stronger and faster.'

An American gold medallist laughed when I asked him whether he dreamt about the Olympics growing up. 'Hah, no, it was a very gradual evolution which started in high school with a little success, not even a lot of success, but enough to keep me interested. Then it was college and a little more success, enough to keep me going and, as sheer luck would have it, we had an amazing college team and a really good coach. It just kind of kept going. Many people in my high school and college and beyond were tremendously talented physically and would run rings around me but they all fell away over time – real life overtook them.' He loved basketball ('I tried like hell to dunk a basketball as a kid but I could barely touch the rim') and tennis as a child ('My real dream was to be a tennis player, this is back when tennis was really big in the US. I played relentlessly and did everything I could to be good at it'). Needless to say, his gold medal wasn't won in either of these sports.

Most young, future Olympians had their heroes but didn't dream that one day they would be up there competing at an Olympics. After all, who actually believes they can grow up to be their idol? Who thinks they'll go through puberty and become a superhero? For most, the dangerous and seductive thought that they might one day be able to compete at the Olympics comes far later, in the late teens or early 20s, once they're well past the foothills of Mount Olympus, having been to an U23 or U21 World Championship and having perhaps won their first senior international vest. Then the cloud clears from the top of the mountain and you can see the summit, still far off, but you can see it. Only then do you start dreaming about it.

Naturals

The second or third question in the local journalist's armoury for the newly anointed Olympian, depending on how early they jump to asking about your medal chances, is 'What made you take up the sport?'

The response is often something about a favourite school coach or a parent who wanted them to try the sport. What Olympians don't tend to say is that they often had a miserable time with the traditional school sports and were ecstatic to find an escape, a sport where they avoided the searing shame of being the last kid to be picked.

I was rubbish at football and, when I was a young teen, too wet for rugby. I was almost always the second last to be picked, just before the immensely fat kid. Revealing my shame to other Olympians I was surprised to find I wasn't alone. In fact, most shared that sentiment.

One silver medallist sums up the comments of many with just a few words, 'I wasn't a natural athlete in school.' Another Olympian, the fencer Nick Bell, echoes my experience. 'I took up fencing at school [aged 13] as a soft option to rugby which I hated. I won the novices' competition at the end of term and it went from there. No more rugby pitches. Ever.'

Even my teenage sporting inspiration, a teacher at my school who'd competed at the Olympics, had it fixed in his teenage mind that he was a sporting failure when he couldn't make the school football team. It took an Olympic medal to persuade him otherwise.

But once most future Olympians have stumbled upon their sport, they discover that they are naturals. Maybe not at the top of their peer group immediately, but in the top tier pretty quickly (it took me a year to reach the higher end of my group). Having developed an image of yourself as a failure at sport after struggling with the two or three popular mainstream games, suddenly discovering a talent is very, very seductive. And addictive.

Dutch volleyball gold medallist Bas van de Goor summed it up: 'I found my motivation at an early age. First I liked the game, then I liked the winning.'

Another Olympian confirmed: 'There's nothing like a bit of early success.'

Fencer, Susie Murphy (Susan Green in her sporting days) was at the extreme end of 'being a natural'. A charming and petite 5'2", and today retired with two 20-something sons, she doesn't look like a triple Olympian. But looks are deceiving. Susie didn't plan to go to the Olympics as a kid but she recalls watching Rome in 1960 aged 11 on a tiny black and white screen, and then watching Tokyo four years later. 'What I didn't realise was four years after Tokyo I'd be [competing] at the Mexico Olympics. I hadn't even started fencing! I was sat watching in 1964 and then four years later was actually in it.'

Susie started fencing at school, at her state secondary modern outside Manchester, which was unusual as fencing at that time was very much a public school sport. 'One of my teachers at school had learnt it in the Army and he decided to get a class going. I didn't like being out on the playground, especially on cold days, so I thought I'd have a bash.' She showed talent, 'and it just kind of snowballed after that.'

'My very first competition was the National Schoolgirls' Championships. If was full of posh schools like Roedean, St Mary's and Benenden. And then I rocked up. And I won it. And everybody thought – who is she? Where's she come from? So I kept at it. I liked winning and I liked the feeling of winning, of being the best. It's addictive. It's a nice addiction. After the schoolgirl championships I went onto the National Championships and then the World Junior Championships in Tehran.'

It's difficult to imagine Western parents putting their 17-year-old girl on a plane to Iran today. 'This was 1967, when the Shah of Persia was still on the throne,' she chuckles. 'It was the first time I'd been on an aeroplane.'

The following year she became the British Senior Women's Champion, aged 17, which secured her place for Mexico City in 1968. She had just turned 18, 'I was the youngest fencer ever to go to the Olympics,' she smiles. Susie went on to Commonwealth gold in 1972 and two further Olympics.

Not all future Olympians rise through the ranks as quickly as Susie did, or have as much early success, but they're normally very good, very early. Multi-gold medal track cyclist Chris Hoy was the second best junior BMX rider in Britain for several years; Steve Ovett set national 800m age records at 15, 16, 17, 18 and 19; British triathlete Sian Brice who competed in Sydney was flying to swimming galas in Ireland from the Isle of Man at the age of 10 and staying with guest families she'd never previously met. By 14 she was running cross country for England; aged 17 she was running 1,500m at the Commonwealth Games and was one of only two junior girls to make the senior 1,500m National Championships final – the other junior being Kelly Holmes.

Why did she get into sport? 'I started swimming and I remember winning a couple of medals and I think that motivated me – I liked it. Once you taste that success you don't want to give it up.'

Olympic gold medallist rower Tom James recalled how success as a team was enormously important to him. 'When I started rowing at 13 or 14 we had a great year group, a great base of friends, and we won everything, which was the catalyst for carrying on. Then we won the J15 nationals, then the Anglo-French match as J16s and you start seeing what's ahead: the incentive of representing Great Britain at the Junior World Championships and beyond.'

Even in individual rather than team events, a buzzing group of young successful compatriots is part of the recipe for Olympic success. Becoming world class in solitude is nigh on impossible. Susie Murphy was joined at her small club in Ashton by Marilyn Holmes who also became schoolgirl champion and went to three World Youth Championships, two with Susie. Table tennis Olympian Matthew Syed recalls in his book *Bounce* how more than half a dozen top players were spawned in his Omega club near Reading. My squad at school contained several Junior World Championship medallists.

Not that being a natural is enough. Huge amounts of work and training are required to unlock the talent. I'd done more than 5,500 hours of training by the time I left school. Even as a teenage schoolgirl Susie Murphy was travelling more than an hour and half each way to train in Ashton-under-Lyne every evening, after her first school coach recognised he had taken her as far as he could and sought out more expertise to allow her to reach her best.

Once you're hooked on success it's difficult to quit. As the giant Josh West says, 'Once you're on the train, it's just going one direction. It is gathering steam and you stay on it. It just totally makes sense. There's not even a consideration that it wouldn't make sense to stay on it. It just builds and builds.'

But before the Olympic train reaches its destination, you've first got to be able to dress the part.

The best Christmas ever

Earls Court, London
7 July 2004

I carefully manoeuvre the other half's Polo in the multi-storey car park adjacent to Earls Court 2 in London. My National Lottery grant hasn't yet stretched to a car but I can't complain, I've bought myself plenty of new kit with my B level grant – £18k courtesy of the all-powerful team manager and last year's medal at the World Championships. And there's no tax to pay. Given we're out of the country for about a third of the year at training camps across Europe, which are all paid for, it goes quite a long way. Particularly as I'm still squatting in my parents' attic and my girlfriend's London flat.

Being an Olympian, or at least an Olympian-in-waiting, is turning out to be quite fun. Naturally the first thing you do is tell your family and friends, who go nuts. A couple of years ago, I went through a similar drill, ecstatically announcing I'd been picked to go to the World Championships. The difference in response is startling, given that from an athlete's perspective you are racing the same opposition. Outside of close friends and family, who are a bit closer to the sport having picked it up by osmosis, many of those you proudly tell you're going to the World Champs respond with subdued congratulations but look a bit sheepish. They seem to be thinking, 'Wow, that hobby that has gotten way out of control. Bit of an unhealthy obsession'.

But tell the same crowd you're going to the Olympics and something very different happens. Eyes widen as the news sinks in, 'I know an Olympian. This will sound great at the pub!'

Turns out no one, sporting geeks and proud parents aside, cares about or watches World Championships, whether archery, cycling, fencing, weightlifting, canoeing or handball. But everyone watches the Olympics.

I rustle through my bag to find my Olympic checklist from the BOA. It's beneath another item of recent post from Powerade. As the official sports drink for the Athens Olympics, Powerade (a subsidiary of Coca-Cola I discover) will be available at all Olympic venues to cater for athletes' 'hydration and fuelling needs'. And, to get future Olympians used to Powerade and help fuel our training, a Powerade card was attached. On the back is the 'Powerade hotline'. Ring it any time and crates of Powerade will be couriered to you next morning, anywhere in the world. Would be more tempting if it tasted any good (the options seem to be electric blue, luminous green or radioactive yellow). We've been using Lucozade for years and will be surreptitiously using their potions and powders at the Olympics – tastes better and no one wants to change their diet and routine now anyway.

Still, just for the hell of it, I got three crates of Powerade couriered to me yesterday. Well, why not? Back to the BOA checklist.

• *Return certificate of dental fitness*
Done. No unexploded dental time bombs to keep me up the night before the final.

• *Medical check up with team doctor ('the results of any medical are confidential to the medical team and will not be communicated to any other person without your consent. If team management have a concern about your health and performance they can ask for medical results or for another medical check. You may still refuse the release of any or all details but this refusal will be reported and taken into account by your team management.')*
Tick. Nervous moments as the Doc listened to my heart and lungs and looked very sombre. Before pronouncing me fine. Turns out he always looks sombre.

• *Submit list of all medicines, vitamins and supplements being taken to Team Doctor*
Also done. Short list.

• *Arrange payment of bills and credit cards*
Credit cards? They haven't seen my credit rating.

• *Sign and return the Team Member's Agreement*
Hmm, will do that later.

• *Attend Olympic kitting out ('preferable to drive if at all possible')*
Here I am at Earls Court 2. I pre-emptively tick it off with relish. Earls Court? It's not the Boat Show. Overkill surely?

On the way up the concrete stairs I'm behind two sporty-looking girls in their 20s, who are chatting excitedly. The first sighting of Olympians from another sport! I feel like I've seen a couple of celebrities and have to resist the urge to stare at them and wonder where I've seen them before. I have to check myself – you're going to be an Olympian too, you idiot, get a grip, they're no different from you. Still, I wonder what they do. I guess hockey or sailing. Not especially tall or short or solidly built.

Not since Christmas Day aged six have I felt such electric anticipation. Back then I'd burst into my parents' bedroom at 5am, buzzing with a sugar high having eaten all the Toblerone in my Christmas stocking. I couldn't wait any longer to unwrap the presents it felt like I'd been waiting an age for. Just like then I don't quite know what I'm going to unwrap, but I'm pretty sure I'll like it.

Inside, there's a hustle and bustle of casually dressed and radiantly fit looking people: more Olympians to be. They are all smiling. It looks like a toothpaste advert. The hall is split into sections – formalwear, sportswear and casualwear, each with a number of tables and counters and discreet corners for trying the kit on. What look like army quartermasters stand behind each table.

First you pick up the luggage. I present myself to the right desk, show some ID and it begins.

'One large suitcase, one large holdall, one rucksack,' barks the man behind the desk as his colleague ticks them off a list. Definitely army guys. All the luggage is in various combinations of red, white and blue with the smart, professional-looking Team GB lion emblem. I resist the temptation to do a little jig.

The lead quartermaster opens the yawningly empty large wheelie suitcase and starts packing things in at speed. 'Alarm clock, check; guide book, check; sun lotions, check; watch, check; sunglasses, check; fan, check.' They continue furiously packing an amazing variety of stuff and ticking respectively. I stand and smile.

The first suitcase is pretty full by the time I'm ushered into the next area by the army guys, who clearly relish ordering around the excitable athletes wandering dopily in a trance-like state of happiness.

The opening and closing ceremony outfits shake me out of my euphoric state. The off-cream jacket looks like something Dr Livingstone would have worn on his treks across Africa. All I need is a pith helmet. The red shapeless polo shirt beneath doesn't help the look, nor the ridiculous hat options – a floppy sunhat or something called a 'poor-boy cap' (can they really call it that?) – a beret-type thing, which looks like something a badly-dressed teenage skateboarder might have worn in the '80s. Made by Roots. Who the hell are Roots? Billions of people might see me in this!

I'm still reeling from the stadium attire when I reach formalwear, the suit for 'official Team GB functions'.

'*This is the suit we'll meet the Queen in after the Games,*' a teammate (who I'll call Jamie) nods at me. As a previous medallist he's enjoying showing the wide-eyed young 'uns the ropes. I see Ben Sherman is the official formalwear provider. OK, at least I've heard of them. You think smart suit – you think Armani or Hugo Boss – you don't think Ben Sherman, but at least they didn't let Roots loose. I bet the Italian team don't have to deal with this.

'*M&S did Sydney,*' Jamie informs me as he slips into the jacket, to mixed reviews apparently.

Then the tailor brings out my suit, already made up from the measurements I sent in last week. It looks rather good. Black with thin gold pinstripes and an embroidered Team GB Athens Olympics crest with thick gold flashing on the breast pocket. I try not to cry in front of my teammate as the tailor helps it onto my shoulders. Close up, I see the pinstripes aren't normal pinstripes but '*Go For Gold*' repeated thousands of times in tiny white gold lettering. Cheesy, but sort of cool. Inside, the lining is red and white silk with little Team GB lions. Amazing. Even Jamie, my teammate who's trying hard not to look too excited, the 'seen it all before' double Olympian, nods approvingly. The suits are slipped into suit bags but it's not over yet. Shiny black formal shoes appear. The inner soles have colour prints of Sydney gold medallists. I'm literally walking in the footsteps of Steven Redgrave and Denise Lewis. Perhaps best yet, three pairs of Olympic boxer briefs, also Ben Sherman. For sizing, I slip one pair on behind a screen, over the top of my civilian underwear naturally. Wow. Very figure hugging and rather package enhancing.

I feel truly Olympian.

And then we're on to the sportswear section. Turns out Adidas is providing all the sportswear for 4,000 Olympians and all the judges and volunteers – 100,000 of them! Much of the training gear is made from 'next generation' breathable, low resistance Lycra stuff called ClimaCool, to deal with the 'particular climatic demands' of Athens's summer. The trainers are also special and 'breathable' to keep my feet from overheating presumably. I'm told to take as many T-shirts as I need. Not wanting to look a gift horse in the mouth and trying to think piously of all the old teammates who'd like one (in reality I just can't get enough kit with the Olympic rings on) I cram my bag with as many tops as will fit. Which is a hell of a lot when it's all made of wisp-thin Lycra.

I'm bubbling with excitement until I pull on the Olympic race gear. My light-hearted euphoria evaporates instantly and I inhale a lungful of fear. Suddenly it all feels very, very real. Then we are given our 'podium tracksuits' to change into and are pointed towards the centre of the room for our official team photos. I feel like a drunk who's had a bucket of ice water tipped over him. Instant sobriety.

While waiting in the queue for team photos (the type you see on press releases and the BBC news website, I realise excitedly, the designer Team GB lion in the background), watching mystery Olympians sit on the stool and smile hopefully at the flash gun, I can't help thinking of all those who didn't make it this far. Schoolmates. Old comrades from Junior European Championships long ago. Mates from the Under 23s. And one athlete who's been in the mix in the British squad all year. Known to all of us (and his mum) by his nickname Chimp, he's loved universally in the squad for his cheeky attitude, humour and optimism, and his total lack of political manoeuvring with the coaches. I think he's the only guy who absolutely everyone likes; everywhere else in the team there are little factions, rivalries and jealousies. In final selection he was stitched up and his place went to an up-and-coming youngster who can bench press almost 200kg – a young freak. Chimp is mid-30s and has fought for years on the fringes of the team, putting off his wedding year after year until he quits the sport so he can 'be a proper husband'. He's strong but not a freak, he's mortal. He trained so hard this year he developed two bulging discs in his back. Our head coach told him, 'What comes with training will go with training'. But it never did really. He's put off a career for more than a decade to try to make the Olympics. What's he going to do now?

Finally it's my turn to sit on the stool and face the camera. Like all the others who've sat before me I find myself wondering what the next few weeks will bring. Will this photo be used alongside a rousing story of victory against the odds? Or alongside a piteously disappointing account of injury or failure to perform on the world stage. Or will it not get used at all? I'm aching to know

– anything for a crystal ball or a divining rod or a sign from above, anything to tell me what the Olympics will hold.

I can't even begin to imagine life after the Olympics. I can just about see ahead to the end of August and the last day of the Games. After that there is just this blackness. I've got an overwhelming feeling that what happens in the next few weeks will decide the course of my life.

Sign up and dress the part

All the athletes I spoke to remember getting kitted out as a welcome light-hearted moment in an otherwise intense build-up. Steve Batchelor, of Los Angeles, Seoul and Barcelona, remembers his first 'kit experience'.

'What I remember from '84 was my Coca-Cola radio. The kit increased definitely. We went to pick it up from the BOA office in Wandsworth, a rabbit warren of little rooms. It was such an exciting day. The kit thing was always quite a big thing. And there are all these rules and regulations. In '84 we had some hockey shoes we really liked, designed by one of our coaches with Clarks. We had to blank out the brand and paint stripes on the side of the shoes.'

Branding is a big deal for big business and there are massive corpo-rations involved with the Olympics who pay hundreds of millions for the privilege. By 1984 athletes had started cutting logos into their hair for extra sponsorship dollars but that was soon outlawed. Tattoos now also have to be covered with T-shirts or make up. Linford Christie must have had very careful legal advice before he put in his Puma-etched contact lenses in Atlanta.

Adidas supplied not only our gear but also kit for the Americans, Greeks and 19 other nations, covering 4,000 athletes in their well-known triple stripe. Greek volunteers and officials received Adidas as well. The sportswear giant also provided more than 1.4 million prod-ucts (including 1,300 balls) for Athens, taking the battle to Nike.

The kit bonanza ensures socio-economic backgrounds are no divide, particularly important in earlier Olympics when funding was hard to come by. Here's a 1960s Olympian: 'It meant everyone, including the athletes who couldn't afford it, everyone was starting off with the same tops and outfits so nobody would suffer not being able to afford something to wear.'

From backroom beginnings in the 1960s and '70s, the kitting out ceremony is a major event for modern Olympians. Here's a Beijing champion:

'You turn up with nothing and leave with £4,000-worth of kit. Ridiculous things like dog tags. Things you're never going to wear outside the opening ceremony, sailor's outfits and hideous shoes. That's when it hits you, what this is about. When you get your kit, that's when you identify with what you're doing. You get your racing kit and you suddenly realise what you're going to be taking part in.'

Nick Bell remembers the need for tailoring, given the extreme physical attributes of Olympians.

'Take fencers: we get one-sided. Your front leg [which you lunge on] is much bigger than your back. And you get the lobster claw arm – your sword arm is huge and the other one is tiny. That's why you have to get measured up so carefully for your suit.'

I remember the tailor wincing after measuring my thighs. And I remember wincing when I read the Team Member's Agreement which we all had to sign, sent prior to the fitting out. We'd been given the heads up it was coming.

All members of Team GB are required to sign the Team Member's Agreement as a condition of their entry and participation in Team GB. The BOA has consulted with the Athletes' Commission and Team Leaders about this document. The agreement will be sent to team members to formally sign shortly after they have been selected.

You sign your Olympic contract, without variation, or you don't go to the Games and frankly, I don't blame the BOA, given all the funds they invest in the athletes and the opportunity the Olympics provides for national embarrassment on a world stage.

The contract details some of the benefits of being a Team GB member: provision of kit, flights ('gold medallists may, depending on availability, receive an upgrade by our sponsor to first class on their return') and insurance, etc; the lengthier obligations of being a member of Team GB (e.g. when to wear certain items of kit, respect for Team GB sponsors, compliance with anti-doping rules, dealing with the media, disclosure of injuries, etc); and the obligations of the Olympic Charter (in order to receive an Olympic accreditation you must agree to abide by the IOC's Olympic Charter).

A 2008 Team GB Olympian remembers a unique clause in the paperwork before Beijing: 'I remember signing that weird contract. That stood out. There was a statement in it about agreeing not to incite political unrest in China.'

Break the rules and you can be legally dropped. Many don't even bother reading it before they sign, given there is no room for negotiation. But once the contract is signed, and you've got your gear, you're on your way. One last stop before the Games. Holding camp.

the expectation

The last stop

Continental Europe, holding camp
10 August 2004

We left the UK several weeks ago now and we won't return until after the Olympics. Back to living out of a bag at another training camp. With all the camps and the international competitions over the last year, Jamie and I have spent more nights rooming with each other than with our girlfriends. We're like a long-married couple, finishing each other's sentences and occasionally pissing each other off and getting in secret strops for the smallest things.

This isn't just another training camp, this is 'holding camp'. The last stop before the Olympics. The idea is to complete your preparations away from home at a quiet off-shore training facility. No journalists asking silly questions, no boyfriends or girlfriends around to keep you up late or fight with or fall in love with, and no friends popping by to have a beer. And none of life's day-to-day stresses – no cooking, no shopping, and no fights with the builders or worries about a leaking washing machine. The camp's within an easy half-day transfer to the Olympic city and at the same altitude and with a similar climate, so our bodies get used to operating at the right temperature and humidity, adjusting to the 'heat stress' like finely tuned car engines. It's like training at the Olympic competition venue but without the Olympics, avoiding distractions, being overawed or just going stale.

The staff at the little hotel look after us. All we have to do is sleep, eat, train and rest. The team manager has been out to test the food and inspect the kitchen several times over the last two years – his nightmare is all of us suddenly going down with E. coli or a stomach bug or something. We religiously disinfect our water bottles every couple of days, to stop bacteria growing on the sugary sports drink residues, and there is a strict no-sharing-of-bottles rule to prevent any nascent infection spreading. Before and after every meal we rub our hands like surgeons with alcohol gel spray. No one is allowed to walk anywhere in bare feet, in case they tread on something sharp and it gets infected. We are not allowed out without suntan lotion – burn badly by mistake and you're dehydrated and sub-par for days. If the team manager could wrap us entirely in cotton wool and keep us like that until the Olympic final, he would sleep a lot better.

Today is our last weight training session. We're not trying to set personal bests and risk anything, but to put the muscles under serious load to maintain our strength for our main sport. The sweat drips off me while I'm doing squats in the heat, the bar straddling my shoulders. I feel so fit, there's an almost sexual gratification to the repetitive straining.

Like the others, I can't help snatching narcissistic glances at myself in the wall mirror. We've each built, moulded and chiselled the clay of our bodies over many years through force of will. Muscles and sinews bulge and strain across shoulders, back and legs. My muscles feel like they want to burst from the skin. My body fat percentage is just where I want it, well under 10 per cent but not low enough to impair the immune system. It strikes me this will probably be the most 'ripped' I'll ever be. I mention it to the half dozen guys lifting and we end up taking photos of each other doing Arnold Schwarzenegger poses. God, we're so vain.

'Something to show the future wife one day, Diesel.'

'Or your kids when you're a proper fat bastard,' I grin at another of the guys, who despite all the training still has a little bit of a tummy on him somehow.

Since we left the UK our digital cameras are permanently at our sides. After dinner many of the boys can be found scribbling in diaries or making soulful video diaries of themselves (haunted looks obligatory). We all want to record this final run in, the most important weeks of our lives, and writing and talking about our fears helps lighten them.

Back in our room I grab a couple of anti-inflammatories for my back from the Team GB wash bag, which is full to bursting with drugs. Approved and legal drugs. The team doctor handed the bags out before we left. Each is filled with approved cold and flu remedies, aspirin, anti-inflammation pills, vitamin C with zinc, that sort of thing. All of us athletes (and the British Olympic Association) are ultra-paranoid of taking the wrong sort of medication and inadvertently failing a drugs test. Take Night Nurse for your cold before bed one night and you're fine. Wake up with it the next day and take Day Nurse – BANG! You're banned! The pseudoephedrine that helps to clear your sinuses is also a gentle stimulant. It helps that all the pills we have are top quality, pharmaceutical-grade stuff. No herbal remedies or dodgy vitamin supplements which could have been contaminated with residues of other powders from a shared production line.

The paranoia has reached new heights since Salt Lake City in February 2002. The colourful Scottish skier Alain Baxter, who had his hair dyed blue and white for much of the winter Games, came third in the slalom and won Britain's first ever skiing medal. Two days after getting back to a hero's welcome in his home village of Aviemore he was called up to be informed he'd tested positive. All because he'd used an American Vicks inhaler which, unlike its British cousin, contains a form of the stimulant methamphetamine. A non-active form of the chemical but that didn't stop the IOC stripping him of his medal.

Makes me feel sick just to think about it. It's one thing secretly taking performance-enhancing drugs and failing a test. A terrible thing to do but hey, at least you might be faster in the interim. It's quite another thing to take Day Nurse and be banned and have everyone think you're a cheating bastard anyway. That own-goal sensation multiplied a million fold.

The athletes' agreement we've all signed reminded me of the number of agencies who are out to test us.

You should be aware that the International Olympic Committee (IOC) will be undertaking pre-competition tests, not only in Athens but at holding camps. The World Anti-Doping Agency (WADA) and

UK Sport are also within their rights to perform tests on any British athlete at any time. BOA bye-law precludes any athlete found guilty by his or her Governing Body or International Federation of any doping offence after 25 March 1992 from being eligible for consideration as a member of Team GB at any future Olympic Games.

The paranoia about a failed test means we all watch our pints at bars like we're about to get date-raped. I've rushed out of two parties when I've smelt some questionable smoke. Passive inhalation of recreational drugs could get you banned from the team. Lucky we don't go to many bars or parties.

Happily for me, as a coffee nut, the caffeine limit has been lifted. Earlier this year WADA announced caffeine is no longer a banned substance. Red Bull must be pretty chuffed about it because they're now sponsoring a couple of guys in the team. The boys have got crates of the stuff with them; they glug down a couple of cans before important training pieces. One of the guys has occasional heart palpitations but tells me he got them for years before anyway.

Along with WADA, UK Sport and the IOC, the sports physiologists also own our bodies. We are all feeling even more like lab rats than usual as the physiological monitoring has stepped up a notch. In the mornings, before breakfast, we hand in our urine samples, weigh ourselves and report on the quality and quantity of our sleep. The urine allows them to keep an eye on our hydration and watch for the protein profile which indicates the dreaded over-training syndrome. Not that it's likely now, as the workload is gradually tapering off.

After each piece of speed work the physiologists (known as the vampires) take blood samples from our ears to review our pace against the levels of lactic acid in our blood. When we're finished they strap us into ice jackets to bring our core temperatures down quickly and to help clear the lactate. It's like being strapped into the inside of a freezer in your underwear when you've been sunbathing all afternoon. There's a kind of unwritten rule in the squad that you don't yelp or puff when it's strapped on. Just suck it up stoney-faced.

The physiologists can't measure our sanity. Some of us are going well in training, quick and confident. Probably an equal number are struggling, working harder than they should to make the pace, and it's those guys (some are friends, some rivals) who are starting to crack up. I can sort of smell this creeping fear of failure, an aura or a vibe around them. It's like an elephant in the room. No one wants to talk about it. Some have gone very quiet; others are sort of manic. I can tell my best mate has been crying in the loos after training and back in the hotel sometimes. Not good for a grown man. Most of the cracking up is kept private and under wraps but there was an unusual public display yesterday afternoon when one of the teams had a big barney and slanging match that started over something insignificant like one of them not carrying their share of equipment after training. It ended when they each stormed off to different points of the compass. Today, thankfully, there's an uneasy peace.

We celebrated our final evening here yesterday with a pizza and a single beer in town. No repeat of the last-night antics from our January altitude camp. We'd had a pretty good party. One of the younger lads (who I'll call Jack), freakishly strong but mercurial, drank a whole Wellington boot of Guinness in a drinking competition with a Swiss guy. The next morning he was missing. We packed his bag for him and tried to keep it quiet over break-fast. The coaches noticed when doing the final head count on the bus before we left for the airport. Just as we pulled away he arrived from his overnighter with a local. We all cheered as he got on, grinning from ear to ear. Even some of the coaches were laughing.

Back in the UK the team manager went totally ballistic. Jack got pulled in for an interview, with the athletes' representative alongside to help arbi-trate. I wish I'd been a fly on the wall. Luckily Jack gave us a blow by blow account after.

'Jack. I understand you were disgracefully drunk,' the team manager eyed him over his spectacles accusingly, waiting for the admission of guilt and pleading for forgiveness.

Jack replied matter of factly, 'Well, I can't have been that drunk, I still managed to …'

'ENOUGH!' The team manager raised a hand urgently before Jack elaborated further on his overnight stay, eyes clenched shut like he was fight-

ing off a migraine. The team manager was rendered speechless and Jack left. The manager almost pulled Jack's Lottery grant which would have made him penniless overnight. If Jack didn't have such a promising physiology I think he would have done. The head coach has also retaliated by introducing a nasty early-morning training session before we leave each camp to disincentivise last-night celebrations, not that one was needed on this camp.

Jamie and I finish packing up in contemplative silence and lug our bags down to the coach. Lucky the big Olympic suitcase is on wheels or half the team would have done their backs. Everyone is wearing the red Great Britain polo shirts. Optional extras are the sleeveless cream jersey and flat cap/gangster beret (depending which way round you wear it). Again, everyone is taking more photos than usual. A couple of the guys are having their photos taken with their arms round the attractive blonde physio, who is enjoying it a tad more than might be professional. Might be a story there when the competition is over.

In a sea of red and cream Chimp stands out in his casual white Nike T-shirt. As an unofficial spare he didn't get invited to visit Earls Court and he's repeatedly refused offers of Olympic kit from the rest of us, even though he's done all the training. He's flying home today. The rest of us are flying to Athens.

The bus is a complex mix of moods. Those who are pleased to have qualified and aren't carrying the weight of medal expectation are buzzing and electric. The real gold medal contenders project quiet confidence. Most of the others, those who know they should be or could be medal prospects, are dark, brooding and silent. The future is weighing heavily on their shoulders.

Whether buzzing or silent everyone is wondering – how will I come back? A laughing stock? A nobody?

A hero?

Searching for perfection

Holding camp is a recent invention. Ask a pre-National Lottery Olympian where they went for their holding camp and you can expect laughter or a quizzical look. I asked Susie Murphy, who fenced at three Games, the last being Montreal in 1976. 'Holding camp?' Susie laughs. 'We just went to the Olympics, matey, and got on with it. You did the best you could.'

For today's Olympic coaches, with budgets and professional athletes who don't have the constraints of a day job, holding camp is seen as a critical final piece of the jigsaw in Olympic performance. Two weeks or so of preparation in a quality venue with the same climate as the Olympic venue and no distractions, leaving the athletes to focus self-ishly 100 per cent on their performance and giving the team managers complete control. On foreign soil, performance directors can manage athletes' diets, ensure total physiological monitoring and give coaches ample time to tinker with final, small, technical changes. Then in the evening there is all the time in the world to make adjustments to equip-ment or conduct video analysis.

Team management sees this monastic final phase as essential to performance, to the extent that when the World Championships of my sport was taking place in the UK, practically in the team's backyard, the squad was taken on a pseudo-holding camp, based for two weeks at an off-roundabout Travelodge, even though we could have driven from home just as easily.

In 2008 British team management established the holding camp for most sports in Macau. I say most sports, because finding international standard two kilometre rowing lakes or three-day eventing facilities within a short flight of the Olympics is sometimes impossible. Rower Josh West said, 'Before Beijing we had a holding camp in the UK, in Caversham, staying in a nearby hotel. And we made the hotel really Olympic in feel as far as we could, with lots of decorations. And we tried to make the whole team feel the Olympic spirit. And then we went to Beijing about 10 days before racing started.'

Before Athens most of us were based in Cyprus (in a five star hotel on the ocean; sure beats a Travelodge). Before Sydney, I had heard good reports about the Gold Coast camp which the team flew out to three and a half weeks before the Games. But where do you go when the Olympics is in your own back yard (and you don't fancy Travelodge)? You fly out to a neighbour. The Australian athletics coach, who was involved in Sydney 2000, gave the UK athletics head coach, Charles van Commenee, some frank advice for the run up to London 2012, 'Don't prepare at home'.

Modern, professional Olympians are used to packing their bags for two weeks and vanishing on training camp. In the run up to Athens I spent between a third and a quarter of the year away at foreign camps or at competitions. It was tough for those athletes with young kids. Plenty of tearful goodbyes at the airport and guilty looks to the wives and girlfriends literally left holding the baby.

Before holding camp, separated often by just a few days' training at home, many of the endurance athletes will have spent a couple of weeks at altitude camp at over 1,500m, to top up their systems with the natural (and legal) answer to blood doping (the misuse of techniques or substances to boost the number of oxygen-carrying red blood cells in the body). With the reduced air pressure of altitude there is less oxygen available and the body responds by increasing the production of a hormone called erythropoietin (EPO). EPO stimulates the body to produce a larger number of red blood cells, which increases the amount of oxygen which can be carried to working muscles, improving aerobic performance. While you're up at altitude the training is miserable. All your split times are well off normal pace because of the reduced oxygen, and you feel weak and out of breath. To make matters worse, while you're slaving in the gym at the top of a mountain somewhere, out of the window skiers and snowboarders whoosh down snow-covered slopes. No fun winter sports for the athletes though for fear of broken legs. While it may be miserable at the time, come down from the mountain and for a few days you're supercharged.

For endurance events like triathlon, which is two hours of mainly aerobic exertion, the extra few per cent from altitude training is crucial to preparations. Here is triathlete Sian Brice, 'We went to altitude camp a lot. Some triathletes, if they came down 24 hours before they'd have an amazing race, but there was mixed evidence on the best interval between altitude training and racing. We'd often drive straight from altitude camp to a race in Lausanne. Once I collapsed during it. I just keeled over and passed out while I was running and it was off to the medical tent for intravenous drips, the works. Two weeks later though I ran an amazing race.'

As well as training camps in South Africa in February and Australia during part of April, the British triathlon squad also had regular training camps in France, where they could go to altitude without going up mountains.

'We used to stay in a spa town called Brides-les-Bains, which is just down from Méribel so in itself it isn't up a mountain. Two French guys, who'd won medals in the biathlon at the winter Olympics, ran this bizarre little bed and breakfast where the rooms on the top floor were all sealed altitude rooms. At night machines would suck the air out of the rooms and take you to up to [the equivalent of] 4,000m. You weren't even allowed the door open for two seconds. You'd wake up in the night and your heart would be thumping and you'd be panting. During the day you had to have your blood oxygen saturation tested every four hours [to make sure you were OK to train]. The idea was to sleep very high and then train both high and low. We could train down at the Albertville running track, do speed work on the bikes in the valley and then later do hill climbing for strength, so it had a bit of everything.'

Happily no longer at altitude, on holding camp the coaches and support team go to great lengths to prepare their charges for the Olympics. From simple stuff, like being made to wear the Olympic racing gear in training to make sure it's worn in (you don't want to be pulling tags off on the starting line or discover it itches you in a distracting place in the warm-up – although the athletes don't like wearing it before arriving at the Olympics for fear of jinxing themselves with injury), to detailed briefings on the conditions in the Olympic city. Here's a few salient points from my briefing note from the BOA.

Greece is one of the smallest countries to undertake the task of organising and hosting an Olympic summer Games. Athens's August temperatures range from an average maximum of 33.2°C and average minimum overnight of 20.7°C. Highs of 41°C have been recorded. Humidity tends to be low to moderate at 50 per cent with regional variations. Average days of August rainfall − 1.7. Dehydration will be an issue. Air quality can be poor, lung function tests are recommended and can be provided by the Olympic Medical Institute.

Some evenings, coaches or psychologists will help run visualisation sessions to prepare their charges. An outsider stumbling in might think they have walked into a cult. Athletes sit cross-legged on their beds with eyes shut while a coach or head doctor (as the psychologists are sometimes known) talks them slowly through their competition at the Olympics, allowing them to imagine and fill in the details with their mind. Then they've been to the Olympics before they arrive.

Sports psychologist Chris Shambrook is a big believer in visualisation, both for physical and psychological benefits.

'Mental rehearsal is a core skill, particularly given the ratio between training and competition. You can mentally rehearse to refine technique and build neural pathways to deliver that technique. When you use visualisation, if you are strapped up to a machine that monitors the electrical activity of the muscles and you imagine a lift in the weights room in great detail, you'll see those muscles firing at a low level. You are laying down and reinforcing the neural [nerve] pathway.

'And you can mentally rehearse to order your thoughts and practise your thinking, to get an understanding of what it's going to look like and feel like when you're actually performing. You can see yourself in different race scenarios, against different opposition and in different environmental conditions and use that to prepare, "In this situation I will look to talk to myself this way."

'Take [British javelin thrower] Steve Backley. While he was injured before 1996 Games [Backley was on crutches for six weeks until three months before the Atlanta Games] he did a lot of mental rehearsal. He won silver.'

Triathlete Sian Brice is also a big believer in visualisation in preparation.

'In triathlon you have to because a lot of things can happen. I mentally prepared myself for three things: (a) the start of the swim is so manic and horrible, you have to get your head round that. In my first ever World Cup, I dived into Stockholm harbour and I didn't really know what I was doing. I got kicked in the face, my goggles filled up and we're in this massive harbour. I just wanted to cry. I was 29 and I was swimming along and all I could think was "I want my Mum! I want my Mum!" In the end it all worked out and I had a really good race. But it was horrible. So I would always massively prepare mentally and remind myself how horrible the swim is.

'Then (b) prepare yourself for something going wrong. What happens if your goggles fall off or you can't get your wetsuit off or you get cramp in transition or you get a puncture on your bike? So you prepare yourself for the things that could go wrong.

'Then finally (c), prepare yourself for the point where it's really hurting, that potentially life-changing moment. Decision-making time. Do I ease off? How much do I want this? My friend put her kids' faces on her bike so when she was finding it really hard she knew what she'd given up. She'd given up a lot of time with them so that was her motivation. Likewise I'd have answers ready when my body asked me how much I wanted this.'

Other evenings at holding camp, ones not sat cross-legged in a trance-like state, are filled with talks from previous Olympic medallists and psychologists to prepare you for the festival of the Olympics. At my holding camp one evening the management unveiled Britain's greatest living Olympian, Sir Steven Redgrave, who must have done the rounds across the British teams. With his huge brooding presence and his track record of five Olympic gold medals spanning Los Angeles to Sydney we hung on his every word. His mantra – do nothing different – is harder than it sounds.

As our psychologist said, 'You want to make sure you exploit the Olympics – don't let the Olympics exploit you.'

Both Sir Steve and our shrink warned us about the Olympic Village. Once you're through security you have a lot of freedom, but that freedom is not a very helpful thing. You suddenly have a dangerous variety of choice that wouldn't be there to tempt you at a World Championships. Should I meet some of the German team for coffee or should I wander to the cinema or should I go to the games room or should I go to the food hall for the fourth time today?

The Village is huge and you can end up walking ridiculous distances without realising it. Then there is the danger of the food hall. It serves any food imaginable 24 hours a day. Sir Steve gave the example of the women's eight in Barcelona, who were struck by a bout of diarrhoea that the team doctor couldn't cure. It turned out that passing the freezers of free ice creams in the Village after training twice a day was just too tempting and they'd each been eating several Magnum ice creams daily, hence the stomach issue. The answer – impose on yourself and your team set meal times and stick to them, and stick to the nutritionist's prescribed diet.

Moving on from food, anecdotes about ultra-competitive athletes getting addicted to video games and staying up all night (the shoot 'em up *Doom* in the 1990s apparently caused at least one Olympian to be sleep deprived on the start line) or straining fingers and thumbs hammering pinball machines, served to warn us off the games rooms.

Then there's the unavoidable distraction of the Village being a circus, the seven-foot-tall basketball players and four-foot-tall gymnasts and people wider than they are tall. And the occasional very famous person.

To amplify the problem of distraction, there is the issue of dead time – with shorter and shorter training sessions and gaps between rounds of competition – suddenly athletes have time on their hands. The psychologist pointed out that time can appear to go more slowly in the Olympic Village while you're waiting for your event, giving more opportunity for an overactive and excitable mind to dream up dangerous distractions.

On holding camp too, boredom can start to be a problem as athletes start tapering down from huge training loads. Too much time to think is a dangerous thing. Our women's team fought back with ultimate time filler – a 6,000-piece 'impossipuzzle' which went on every training camp with them. Unrolled from its travelling tube in the hotel lounge on the first day of each camp and rolled back up lovingly, a few more pieces in place, at the end, the puzzle built up a lot of air miles. By the time Athens finished it was about three quarters done. Fiendishly difficult and strangely addictive. But pointless? No, a carefully-chosen strategy for keeping sane and not over-thinking what lay ahead.

Josh West elaborated on his planning for dead time. 'What did we do? Watched lots of movies and did a lot of reading. Basically anything to distract myself. That was always my strategy for World Championships and other big competitions. By the time you get to the Olympics you have plenty of experience of the Worlds. Tapering down, the training load coming off, the pressure coming on and the dull time coming on because you're not allowed to do anything else. So over the years I became very good at using entertainment, reading and DVDs, to distract myself. In the run up to Beijing one of the guys bought a video camera before altitude camp and we made two videos. One was 'Go West' – except that it was 'Go East'. The other was a spoof of 'My Way' and we all dressed up in funny shit. It's on YouTube. That was a good distraction.'

'Rowing My Way' does indeed have some amusing outfits (including a lemon mankini, spoof cowboy, gauntleted chest-waxed superhero and mad scientist) and shows a closely-knit team. Silly outfits are a bit of a recurring theme on training camp. A Sydney Olympian I spoke to said on holding camp her coach ordered an Elvis party, with each athlete having to fashion an outfit of the great man and provide some cabaret.

Apart from making spoof music videos, athletes do other strange and sometimes disgusting things when bored on camp. One athlete trying to make Sydney was renowned for eating or drinking whatever his unfortunate roommates happened to leave out. An irritating trait. Athletes love their food and many bring favourite biscuits, chocolate bars or other titbits lovingly from home.

To teach him a lesson after a particularly bad spate of eating others' treats, his roommate left out a booby-trapped pint of orange juice. It had pulpy bits and a little extra syrup of his own creation, well stirred in. True to form, while the other man was in the shower the gannet drank down the entire pint whilst watching Eurosport. Emerging from the shower to see the empty glass of special orange juice and a smug-looking gannet, the roommate burst into tears of laughter and eventually confessed to the trick. In retaliation, later on that evening the gannet inserted his roommate's toothbrush where the sun doesn't shine and then put the toothbrush back in the glass by the sink. He didn't tell his roommate for a week.

Practical jokes and the making of spoof videos can help lighten the pressure, because at holding camp each session has to count. As a bronze medallist, who was always fighting injury, told me, 'There was never enough time to prepare – time was our enemy. You've got to make improvements every day and take the most from every moment. I never felt that it was waiting, I just felt that it was coming too quick and there were too many things still to put right and perfect, and you're never quite there.'

When things are going well, confidence starts to develop and a momentum starts to build which can carry through to a great Olympic performance. But when training is going badly, holding camp can get suffocating. There's nowhere to hide, only the fear that soon you'll be embarrassed on the international stage in front of all your loved ones. Here's one Olympian before Athens:

'I do remember on holding camp deeply having the feeling that we're not going to do well. We'd totally lost faith in our coach. We did some race pace work one session and when we finished he was adamant it was really good. I went into the toilets and cried because I knew it was shit. I was getting overwhelmed with it. Another day we were doing some video analysis and it got to the worst guy who was really temperamental. The coach had been slagging everyone off but when it got to this guy he was like, "That's how I want you to do it". You could see what the coach was doing but it killed the rest of us.'

As you might have guessed, the results weren't good.

For team sports like hockey, holding camp provides the opportunity to select the starting line up. Steve Batchelor of the British hockey team went to three.

'In 1984 it [selection] was so last minute, thanks to the Russian boycott, we didn't go on holding camp. In 1988, before Seoul, we had a couple of days in Hanbury Manor, the golf club, with our wives and girlfriends. Then we went to Hong Kong for a week. In Hong Kong, Roger Self, the manager, told me to go and warm up Ian Taylor, the goalie. When he did that I knew I wasn't going to be first choice on the pitch in Seoul. I started whacking balls at the manager from the other end of the pitch. I was fuming but he didn't say anything. Then in the Olympic Village about two days before the first match, he called me into his room and made me sit down. He said, 'What was all that about in Hong Kong, Batchelor?"

"I know you're not going to pick me."

"No, because you're not playing as well as you can do. But I will put you on in the first game and, if you play well, you'll be first choice."'

After that game, Batchelor became first choice. 'Yep, Roger was a real slave driver, but a soft guy underneath. Now he's a very successful businessman. We had a love hate thing but he made me tick. Some people need you to shout at them to make them play. For me that didn't work. I needed to be told I was good and brilliant and stuff. And that's when I performed.'

When I spoke to Steve, the England cricket team had just returned from the Australian Ashes tour in early February, having flown out with the nation's hopes on their shoulders five months earlier, in October 2010. Three days after returning from the Australian tour they left for the Sri Lankan Cricket World Cup, where the team was beset with injuries both physical and mental, with all rounder Michael Yardy flying home in late March, before the Cup ended, citing depression. The Olympics doesn't demand quite as much continuous time abroad but as Steve says, 'You start to understand why the cricketers are falling apart and are glad [their tour] is over. You're on holding camp a week, then in the Olympic Village a week before competition starts, then you're there another two weeks. It's a long time to be out of a suitcase. Some love it, but you're still quite pleased when it's over, when you're home.'

Being away from friends and family for extended periods is just one of the sacrifices that Olympians are obliged to make. The question in every athlete's mind on holding camp – will the Olympics make all the sacrifice worthwhile?

Sacrifices

To get to the Olympics you've got to be crazy, on a variety of levels. No normal, sane, rational or balanced person would sacrifice enough to get there. Let's take the example of fencer and doctor Nick Bell in his preparation for the Montreal Olympics.

'In the run up to Montreal I was doing a "one-in-three" house job in a district general hospital in Ilford, which meant one week I'd do one night a week, the following week two nights and every third week I'd do the weekend as well. It was before the European time directive. So I'd do 80 hour, sometimes 110 hour weeks. The fencing nights were Monday, Wednesday, Friday and I'd do fitness training and circuits on top of that.

'So some weeks I'd go in [to the hospital] Monday morning 9am, finish about 6.30pm and drive into central London to train. Tuesday I'd be in [the hospital] 9am, do all day and all night, snatching two or three hours' sleep, and then do all day Wednesday. I'd finish at 6pm and drive into central London to go fencing again, having had two hours' sleep and I'd wonder why I wasn't very good. Then I'd go back in Thursday morning, do Thursday all day and all Thursday night. Then start again Friday morning and I wouldn't come out until 6pm Monday evening, when I'd go fencing. It really was draconian. Once in a flu epidemic, when I was really busy, I got five hours' sleep over three nights, total.'

I looked shocked when Nick talked me through his pre-Montreal programme. I suddenly realised I had it easy being full time on the National Lottery's ticket. Surely it was desperately tempting to head home Wednesday evening after all night and all day at the hospital, to see family or friends or just sleep?

Nick replied, with an enthusiastic glint in his eye and a hint of the mad professor, 'We were young and fit. It was fun! You have limitless energy when you're young. You wouldn't do it if you didn't enjoy it.'

A French Olympian I spoke to echoed the point. 'In my opinion I made no real sacrifice. The sport was my passion. I was 24. I was a student, no children, and except for the last six weeks I was never far from home for very long.'

Nick continued, 'Looking back I don't know how I did it. The training regime was crazy for Montreal. Sometimes I'd get so overtired and manic but that's how it was. You just take it on the chin. There's a difference nowadays with a lot of these sports professionalising and regimenting and taking the fun out of things. We were the manic amateurs really. If you professionalise it, it rather loses its sense of humour.'

So Nick sacrificed sleep and time and almost everything else in the run up to Montreal. Susie Murphy, another fencer, was still at school in the run up to Mexico City in 1968, so her sacrifices were different.

'I was spending all my time going up and down to competitions, getting the points I needed to qualify for the Olympics. I remember the headmistress at my school called me in with my parents coming up to A-level time, just before the Olympics. She said, "You're bright enough to go onto university or do fencing, but you're not clever enough to do both. So it's sports or studies". Well, the Olympics was around the corner so it was a no brainer for me. I decided to go for the sport and that's the path I followed. But it stood me in good stead. Even though I didn't go to university, going to the Olympics has opened so many doors for me. So I don't think I came off badly. It was a good decision. I worked on the basis that you can always go to university later in life if you chose to, but you can never recapture going to the Olympics.'

An American Olympian I spoke to summarised his sacrifices in social terms. 'My biggest sacrifices? Time with my loved ones; family, girlfriends of the time. Not being able to commit to seeing people. Never seeing my parents for Thanksgiving.'

I went to university but, with training for my sport, missed out on what would be recognised as all the traditional student fun. No endless cups of tea watching *Neighbours* or *Home and Away* in a dressing gown. No getting into unusual music. No experimenting with drugs. Not much experimenting with other students. Very few all-nighters. Missing some lectures, sleeping through others. Not being able to understand the lectures I did stay awake in, having missed the previous half dozen. No time for fellow students who weren't into my sport. A life on the fringe of student life during the years that are popularly espoused to be the best of your life. After uni, it was the missing of birthdays, stag parties and weddings that hurt the most. The social milestones in life which are talked about for years after; conversations you can never join in.

A British Olympian from Beijing did manage to get to her sister's wedding, but only just.

'My sister got married while I was away on training camp. Because it was 2005, the first year in the cycle up to Beijing, I was given a special dispensation and allowed a whole day-and-a-half off training. I flew back at six o'clock on the morning of the wedding. It's those sorts of things that you realise you miss out on. But in general I felt that I was really lucky to be given an opportunity to do something like this; to do what I wanted to do.'

Triathlete Sian Brice highlighted the lifestyle sacrifices made by some of her competitors, who took altitude training one stage further and brought the mountains home with them.

'A few of them sleep in hypoxic altitude tents every night. They do everything they can to be the best in the world. I was given one but I couldn't sleep in it, the noise was horrendous. We had it in our bedroom for a week but I got rid of it. Maybe if I was totally committed to the cause I'd have given it longer but my sleep is so important and my husband might have divorced me. They're not the most romantic of things.'

And then there is all the physical pain you have to go through. My squad did 'three-three-twos'. We'd do three sessions Monday, three Tuesday and then two hard sessions Wednesday (it was really four-four-twos if you count Pilates and core stability training); then three sessions Thursday, three Friday and two Saturday; then normally two again on Sunday. Every month or so we'd have a day off. On training camps we did up to five sessions a day, sometimes at altitude. I wouldn't think it was physically possible if I hadn't seen it done. The human body is an amazing thing – beat it up by progressively overloading it weight-lifting, sprinting or with other strenuous exercise and it repairs itself, with muscles growing larger and stronger. But pushing the body to overload each time hurts, a lot, and training at that level suppresses the immune system so you are forever on the edge of illness and the dreaded post-viral fatigue and over-training syndrome. Each of us was always nursing an injury or two. Bones, joints, tendons, ligaments, skin, soft tissue or muscles – there's a lot that can go wrong with that much training. You might think with all that exercise you feel fantastic? Sadly, you're generally too knackered and aching to enjoy your supercharged, super-broken, body.

Here's a taste of what Sian Brice's training schedule looked like. 'I'd swim two hours most mornings. Then come home and have breakfast. Then I'd go for a two to three hour bike ride. Then have something to eat and a break. Then I'd do a running session for an hour in the evening. Then three times a week I'd go to the gym straight after the run. So five days a week, Monday to Friday I'd do all three sports and I added three gym sessions as well, doing weights and plyometrics (jumping/skipping/throwing medicine balls) and a lot of Pilates. On Sunday we'd do a long bike, perhaps four hours, and do a run straight after the bike, and then just swim for an hour at low intensity. I'd do the intense stuff on the run because if I did too many miles I'd get injured. I would always have a full day off on Saturday but some people did an extra swim.'

It's tiring just reading that, let alone doing it week after week after week. Her weekly mileage?

'Probably 35km of swimming a week. I was a low mileage runner, I'd do 40km running, mostly of reps on the track and maybe one pretty hard 50-minute threshold run. I didn't really do any steady running. Then we would do a couple of hundred miles on the bike.'

That's a lot of pain, even in the sun of warm-weather training camps. Sometimes it seemed like pain for pain's sake in the men's squad.

'On our camps in South Africa, Simon Lessing, who was legendary in triathlon in the '90s would lead the cycling pack. He'd have all the young, up-and-coming triathletes sitting behind him. He'd just go as hard as he could until they all blew off the back, one by one. It was a hard knock school of learning. Harden the fuck up or get out. It used to drive me mad. That way of training was totally unscientific and unproven but it was his way of toughening the kids up. Have you heard of the Velominati? It's a cycling website with all these bizarre etiquette rules. Some of them are amusing, some are serious. Rule number 5 – Harden the fuck up.'

Legendary Australian triathlete coach Brett Sutton, who trained a number of Sian's competitors, lived by rule number 5. Sian comments, 'The man is a lunatic. Take one of his girls. I raced her at one World Championship back when she was a terrible swimmer. She'd get out of the water 50th [last] and then work her way up – she was a good biker. So Brett trained her. They would do all their normal training and then every night he would make her do 5km of swimming by herself and every length he corrected her stroke. So he'd stop her at the end of each 25m length and he'd correct her stroke for like 200 lengths. You've got to admire his staying power as well. And that would be on top of her normal day's training. A year later she got out of the swim in the first pack of athletes and went on to win the World Championships. She stopped a year or so later.'

Thankfully, though, as well as the athletes' muscles gradually responding to training, the awareness of pain in athletes gradually adjusts too. Here's Olympic gold medallist rower Tom James:

'Pain? A lot of it is perception. That's something I've learnt over the years. I used to absolutely hate it. I couldn't understand sitting on the rowing machine for an hour. But now that I've learnt how to manipulate my own endorphins, the perception of pain is different.

'Music is a very obvious way to trick your mind into ignoring the pain. There's medical research on it. Throughout the season I'll have one soundtrack, with about 25 songs or something. It starts off with an aggressive, high beat sort of song. So you start the ergo [rowing machine] in that frame of mind. You attack it. Having the music distracts you from the pain and you get into a rhythm and you keep pushing on. When they take the music away, or there is other music playing in the gym, I find that really pisses me off.'

And training in a committed team makes the pain so much easier, to the point where the pain is almost fun.

'The mood of the squad influences pain. You're surrounded by other people's hormones and the atmosphere [they generate]. Training can be tough through the winter but if you're in a team which is successful, it's uplifting and positive, so when you're doing the training that has a real impact. If you're negative and sad, and you let yourself get down in the training, it's so much harder.'

Olympians sacrifice their bodies to the training and they also hand over their bodies to others – physiologists and drug testers. Your body is no longer your property. On training camp in particular the vampire physiologists are at you with their needles and vials. My experiences of lactate testing, heart rate monitoring, urine testing and the use of ice jackets or ice baths are commonplace. Back in the UK, Olympians are fully tested several times a year in the lab of the British Olympic Medical Centre. From the outside, the functional and unlovely box of a building on the outskirts of the car park of Northwick Park Hospital doesn't look like much. Inside though, the testing rooms full of wires, tubes, breathing apparatus and sports equipment (treadmills, stationary bikes, rowing machines) and buzzing, motivated physiologists, nurses and doctors, betrays the same high performance mentality of much of the rest of the revitalised Team GB. That said, no athletes particularly enjoy the testing, apart from the rare one or two who are breaking physiological records. Doing a series of increasingly tough work-outs whilst strapped up to wires, heart rate monitors and tubes, and breathing hard through a tight face mask which gradually fills up with spit as you strain and sweat isn't that fun. But afterwards you do get cool graphs of oxygen utilisation and lactate generation, and statistics about lung capacity and VO_2 max (a measure of the body's maximum oxygen uptake which is a better measure of aerobic performance than lung capacity), which are fun to quote to friends who have no idea what you're talking about.

I thought we had it bad. The triathletes had it worse, as Sian Brice told me.

'I was physiologically tested since I was about 15 or 16-VO_2 max and things. We'd go to Northwick Park too, at the BOMC. Triathlon had a very scientific approach. Our performance director Greg Millet was very 'cover all bases' and we worked with sports scientists like Greg Whyte, who now does celebrity stuff [he trained David Walliams, for his Channel and Thames swims and Eddie Izzard for his multi-marathons]. So we were physiologically tested a lot – lung capacity, VO_2, lactate tolerances – at different cycling and running speeds, and in the pool they'd take blood from your ear.

'To get the whole picture you need the core temperature as well, so you ran with a thermometer up the backside. It adds to the data. Relatively I didn't do that well in lab tests, I was always more of a performer [outside]. If I lived by the numbers I could have got quite down sometimes. I did the tests because you're expected to but I actually then went out and raced and completely forgot about them.'

As well as handing your body over to the physiologists, the dope testers, both international like WADA and the IOC, and domestic governing bodies, can arrive randomly any hour of the day or night for a urine sample. International athletes have to submit forms giving details of their expected movements months in advance (the testers can pounce on you on honeymoon if they want) and give precise details of where they'll be for an hour each day. Most choose their flats between 6am and 7am and then have panic attacks when they pick up a new beau and end up staying at their place. The thought of a no-show failed test for a one-night stand makes athletes' blood run cold.

Perhaps elite training pushes athletes towards being manic obsessive. Perhaps those with manic obsessive traits became elite sportspeople. Either way, all athletes hand over their mind as well as their bodies to a greater or lesser extent in the search for Olympic greatness. You've got to be sufficiently unbalanced to want it badly enough. Some are on the edge of mental illness, others over the edge.

Athens hero Kelly Holmes, who took gold in the 400m and 800m, has been admirably public in talking about how she was hit by depression when contending again with old injuries, a little over a year before the Olympics. This led to self-harming with Holmes cutting herself with scissors for each day she was injured. Research around the psychology of injury in elite athletes has shown it has parallels to the grieving process, with the cycle of denial, then anger, before depression and, eventually, acceptance.

Sian Brice saw some unusual behaviour in women's triathlon. 'I saw previous World Champions get pretty screwed up and hating it by the end. It wasn't worth the medal. A few became anorexic. Some coaches would pressure them and say, "It's all power to weight ratio". It's amazing the number of girls who don't eat enough on that kind of training and screw up their metabolism. Then they stop and they get really fat. It should be the time you eat whatever you like. The day before the Olympics in Sydney, one of the girls just ate apples, five of them, trying to lose weight for the race. Another was obsessive about her food. She'd do stuff like not eat meals [in public] but then eat a can of cold baked beans in her room. She was obsessive about lots of things. She would train weirdly. When we were on camp and we had all day to train she would still set her alarm for 5am and go for her run. Another would demand a separate swimming lane because she wasn't quite as good a swimmer. She'd train hard on the easy days and be like, "Oh, I beat you today" and then drop out in the hard sessions and start crying.'

Another common theme of sacrifice is that of Olympians' families, who strive to help them achieve their goals. To make it in sport you need others to sacrifice their time, and often money, for you to make it. I didn't speak to a single Olympian who didn't recognise the huge burden they were to their parents when growing up. My parents spent thousands of hours at weekends and week-nights, driving me to and from training and to races across the country, and spent thousands of pounds on coaching, training camps and kit (and sating my excessive appetite!). Chris Hoy's saintly Dad spent entire weekends (often including much of the night) driving a teenage Hoy between BMX competitions across England and Scotland in a converted camper van, which allowed his son to sleep in the back.

Like his father before him, Steve Batchelor's son, Tom, plays for the England U19 hockey team, which means lots of driving to training camps and hotels and, of course, expense. 'It is costing me a fortune him playing for England, it's ridiculous. The U21s start getting looked after [financially], but [at U19s] I reckon it costs me a couple of grand a year for him to play for England. Of course you wouldn't not do it but it's got to come from somewhere.' And even being selected into the senior team doesn't make you financially comfortable, 'If you look at the [senior] England boys I think they're getting fifteen grand a year now; they were on twenty-one. If you actually look at that, it's not a lot. With accommodation, travel, food, I don't know how they do it.'

Before Lottery funding it was even worse. As one former Olympian said, 'That was the toughest thing when I was competing, I was constantly, constantly broke.' Even as recently as the mid-1990s it was difficult. In my sport, world medallists were paying their own way to World Championships.

Just occasionally, sport does pay very well, outside the traditional ranks of Premiership footballers. Simon Lessing, the English triathlete who was untouchable for much of the 1990s and was expected to win gold at Sydney (eventually he came ninth) was paid something like £1m for Nike endorsements, as the sport of triathlon was taking root in the UK as it came across from America. The majority of the Olympians, however, survive on much more modest means, often with parental support, and would earn much more if they chose a different career over their sport.

As the days of holding camp tick by, seemingly far too fast, just occasionally the fog of the impending Olympics lifts and you try to glimpse life beyond the Games; a seemingly halcyon life of sleeping in, parties, friends' birthdays and family gatherings. A fantasy life of earning a proper salary, not leeching from your family, and doing whatever you want, whenever you want. No more destroying your body, so that it grows back stronger, and being so obsessed you put your mind and relationships at risk.

When finally you pack your national team bags to travel to the Olympic city you know the sacrifices are nearing an end and that they have already partly paid off. Many others put in 99.9 per cent of the effort and pain but didn't get this far. Soon you will have to decide whether to take another spin of the Olympic roulette wheel, staking four more years of sacrifice. Firstly though, it's time for the Olympics.

the reality

Going up in the world

Athens
The British Ambassador's Residence
11 August 2004

The Ambassador, Sir David Madden, is a cordial, ruddy-cheeked guy, with a gift for talking to anyone. Goes with the job. He even managed to smile and look genuinely amused when Jamie, the loveable fool, emerged from the crowd with a small silver tray bearing a neat pyramid of Ferrero Rocher and posed for photos with his long arm round the Ambassador's shoulders.

The thick, cream invitation to the team function was one of the treasures awaiting our arrival. Pleasingly stiff and covered with a bewildering array of initials, insignias and italic fonts. We also received voting forms for the IOC Athletes' Commission elections. A range of multi-gold winning legends, like Sergey Bubka, have been put forward by their own national Athletes' Commissions. Matt Pinsent is our man. Having lost out by one vote in Sydney, the BOA is pressing us to get to the Village and vote for him ('With London bidding for the 2012 Olympic Games it is important that all athletes support Matthew's re-election'). Only a legend among legends will succeed. I'm competing at the Olympics but I feel childlike next to these heroes.

The final item making up the welcome pack was our quarter-inch thick Olympic manuals, which include the details of every competing athlete – their weight, age, height, photo, etc. Everyone flicked through them avidly in this order:

1. Check for yourself to make sure it's not all a dream.

*2. Find the biggest and the tallest mutants (one French judo guy is 200kg –
   none of my bad taste French jokes around him).*

*3. Peruse at leisure for attractive boys or girls, to suit personal taste, for when
   the competition is over.*

*I scan the view across the residence for any of my number 3 selections. None in
sight, but the residence itself lives up to the high expectations set by the invitation
and is surprisingly grand in these post-colonial times. White marble everywhere, Grecian pillars, coats of arms, Union Jack flying and a large garden
which is filled with athletes in Go-For-Gold pinstripe suits, local bigwigs
and dignitaries, Tessa Jowell our Secretary of State, a couple of Greeks in
traditional folk costume and even a few near-retirement, British army types
in sand-coloured formal dress uniform dripping in gold braid. Somewhere in
the morass is Princess Anne, titled in the invitation as 'Her Royal Highness
The Princess Royal, British Olympic Association President and International
Olympic Committee Member'. No doubt she's talking horses.*

*There was a three-line whip on attendance at the event, it being the only
function which all Team GB athletes in Athens are required to attend. Given
how proud and excitable all the guests look in their posh team suits, the whip
probably wasn't needed. Everyone is clearly feeling pretty VIP; prestigious
venue, dedicated motor-coach with police outriders, special and, occasionally,
famous fellow guests.*

*This is our first significant social interaction with other types of athlete and
the differences are eye opening. The gymnasts are mostly tiny little schoolgirls
who've just finished their GCSEs. This whole thing is overwhelming enough
for me in my mid-20s, I don't know how they're managing as kids. I guess
they've been training and performing at such high levels since before they even
reached puberty that in their arena they perform as little automatons; away from
the parallel bars and at a social event on foreign soil, their youth and innocence
radiates from them. The older one of their little gaggle, still not 20, acts like a
mother hen, keeping them together at all times and watching for predators.*

*The divers are tiny too, but more lightly built than gymnasts whose frames
hint at sinewy strength. The synchronised pairs walk around together as if*

*linked at the hip. I get a great photo of a 6'10" rower with the 5'1" divers,
the top of their heads just reaching the embroidered badge on his suit breast.*

*At the garden bar I order an orange juice from the immaculate bar girl and
resist the olives, peanuts and other nibbles. No butter-dipped balls of lobster
or other finger food for fear of food poisoning. No booze either. For most of
us anyway. The guy next to me is of average height and build and is making
rapid progress through the ice buckets full of bottled beers. Must be one of the
support staff. Fair enough, why shouldn't he enjoy himself?*

'What brings you here, mate?' I ask, curiosity getting the better of me.

'On the hockey team.' I almost spray orange juice over him in surprise.

*I retreat back to my crowd. All the talk is of the host nation finishing
Olympic preparations on time … just. Some of the roads which will host
Paula Radcliffe's marathon were finished just two days ago. The IOC must
have been biting their nails. Having made the impossible threat six months ago
of moving the 2004 Olympics back to Sydney (surely ruining thousands of
pre-booked holidays and wasting billions of investment from the host nation
in the process), the IOC eventually backed the Greeks to get it sorted.*

*On first impressions it looks like they have. The international airport
was half full of 'Athens Welcomes the World' banners covered with the
motto 'Welcome Home', harking back to the Olympics' ancient heritage.
The other half of the airport was full of shiny corporate adverts from the
official Olympic sponsors (of which I counted at least three tiers – 'Part-
ners', 'Sponsors' and 'Suppliers'). Sugary drinks, credit cards, fast food and
IT – all the stuff of Olympians.*

*After a nice welcome speech by the Ambassador, a big team shot of the
hopeful-looking athletes is orchestrated in the Ambassador's garden (gymnasts
to the front – rowers to the back). It reminds of me of our graduation photo at
uni – all the fresh graduates standing awkwardly, wondering what life has in
store. Our future is much more immediate, only the next three weeks matter.*

*All too soon the welcome distraction is over and we're ushered back on the
coaches. A pensive mood seems to hang over each of us as we speed along in
the outside lane of one of the city's main arteries, past long lines of stationary traffic. The Olympic lanes, designated by the Olympic ring insignia every*

30 yards of tarmac (no wonder preparing for an Olympics costs billions), are only available for officially accredited vehicles. The rest of the city's drivers curse and swear in the heat as we whistle by, again feeling like VIPs (actually, thinking about it, here we really are VIPs!). I wonder how much the official Olympic vehicle accreditations are trading for on the black market. Without one you're going nowhere.

Wistfully looking out of the window I see central Athens is a continuation of the airport; billboards covered in official Olympic advertising everywhere. HP, Coca-Cola, all the big boys. And the bloody Olympic mascots. What's the point of them? Soft toy sales. Must be.

And the host country's national hero stares down nobly from posters all over. Greek sprinter Konstantinos Kenteris, reigning 200m Olympic champion, is without doubt the face of the Games. Can he surprise world athletics twice? When he won in Sydney it was so unexpected the officials hadn't even organised a Greek/English translator to be on hand for press interviews. His coach had to step in. I don't blame them, I remember him coming last in the European Indoor champs just six months before his gold.

I feel a little better, with schadenfreude. If I feel like I'm drowning under a rising tide of pressure, it's nothing next to what Konstantinos must be feeling, with the host nation's Olympics on his shoulders.

Welcome to Olympics PLC

There is a tangible buzz in the arrivals hall of the Olympic city airport before a Games begins and a nervous excitement and curiosity as Olympic teams eye each other in their respective lurid tracksuits. As spotless and beautiful as an airport interior could ever be (Olympic officials clearly subscribe to the ideal that first impressions count), this is when the concept of Olympics PLC hits home. The Olympics is big business, not just a sports meet. The ancient Olympics honoured Zeus, the King of the Gods. In the arrivals hall of a modern Olympic city you could be forgiven for thinking we hold it to honour the Gods of sportswear, fast food and printing equipment.

As you stroll across the gleaming marble, the Olympic mascots make an unwelcome appearance, eyeing you from the walls of the airport. We have the French to thank for infantilising the ultimate achievement in Olympians' lives, mascots being a tradition ever since the 1968 winter Olympics in Grenoble. And we have London design agency Iris to thank for Wenlock and Mandeville, the one-eyed penis monsters of London 2012, available in 30 different varieties of cuddly toy and expected to generate £15m for the organising committee. On second thoughts, that's £15m less tax that I'll have to contribute towards so perhaps I like the cycloptic duo after all.

Even more prevalent than the mascots is the Olympic city logo. London's controversial stylised 2012 reportedly cost £400,000 to design, a statistic that has become a political plaything but will be a forgotten insignificance on the night of the closing ceremony – should the Games be viewed as a success. Of course, if the Games are a 'failure', it will be one of many monstrous and ridiculous sums.

Heading through the airport, snatches of the official Olympic album waft through the air. For Athens, EMI released *Unity* as the official album of the Games, with contributions from Sting, Moby and Avril Lavigne. Not a patch on the memorable Freddie Mercury and Montserrat Caballé union, 'Barcelona', which lit up the 1992 Olympics.

With all the official logos, mascots, tag lines, sponsors and music, for a minute you could forget there's sport involved. Then you pick up your accreditation.

One veteran of the Beijing Olympics, recalling his first impressions on landing in Olympic city, told me, 'I remember arriving at the airport and just being totally amazed at how it was transformed into this Olympic gateway. The entire airport had been built for the Olympics which drove home the scale of the whole event. You don't go through normal arrivals; you get funnelled through an Olympic arrivals procedure and you get your accreditation when you go through.'

Accreditation is the key to the whole Olympic city, the vital pass that proves you really are an Olympic athlete and not some fit-looking supporter trying to get into the Olympic Village for a nose around. The different grades and types of accreditation dictate which parts of which venue you're allowed into, the most sought after being the 'access all areas' IOC super-accreditation. An athlete losing his accreditation is the stuff of the performance director's nightmares.

My team manager's headmasterly speech was drilled into me.

'DO NOT LOSE IT. They give it to you on a string for a reason. Wear it at all times. You need it to eat, you need it to use the Olympic transport, you need it to get into the Village, you need it to train and you need it to compete. If you forget it or lose your accreditation on the way to your Olympic final, YOU WILL MISS YOUR OLYMPIC FINAL.'

I think he was exaggerating for effect in the last part, I'm pretty sure arrangements could be made, but he still scared us all rigid and our accreditations were glued to us for the whole Games.

After the magic passes are handed out, it's off to the Olympics. Unless you're Olympic gold medallist Tom James in Beijing.

'My first interaction with the Chinese was the bureaucracy. I left my passport at the accreditation point and I followed all these GB people onto the airport shuttle, which transports visitors between terminals, you get off one side and people get on the other. I realised at the end I'd left my passport, so I decided to get the train back and pick it up. The doors closed. Nothing happened. People are outside waiting to get on. Five minutes go by. The doors opened and these armed officers got on to usher me off. They wouldn't let me ride the train back to go back and pick up my passport. My first experience of Chinese protocol – they'd been told people are only allowed one way. There was no one around of high enough authority to make the decision to allow me to get the train back. It was ridiculous.'

Eventually, the athletes do escape the airport and eagerly suck up the sights and sounds of the Olympic city on the way to their accommodation. Even the air in Beijing was a feast for the senses.

Tom James described it, 'It was like walking around in someone's armpit. It was just really sweaty and smelly. I thought my asthma was going to be bad. You heard scare stories that the smog particles were big enough to damage your lungs. There were people wearing these masks over their faces.'

The Olympians only get to inhale a few lungfuls of the city's air before being shepherded through tight security and onto air-conditioned buses which are religiously swept for bombs. It's this first experience of ultra-high security which brings home to the newly-arrived athletes that they, and their Olympics, are potential terrorist targets. As the bus pulls away, into the Olympic dedicated fast lane, it's impossible not to think of Munich and the killing of the 11 Israeli athletes by the Black September. The athletes put it to the back of their minds. As the team psychologist says, control the controllables.

Next stop, the Village.

Village people (part 1)

From the outside, with its high wire fences and armed guards, the Olympic Village looks like a prison. Occasionally it actually is. The winter Olympics of Lake Placid 1980 used a newly-built medium-security prison, the Adirondack Correctional Facility. Not very homely, but at least very secure. The Lake Placid Games was otherwise notable for having the first live Olympic mascot, Rocky Raccoon. Unfortunately the excitement was too much for Rocky who died shortly before the competition started.

Behind the fences, scanners and guards walk the supermen and superwomen of the next two weeks. Mortals need not apply. Inside, the superheroes are split into two tiers. The few medal contenders and favourites. These are the legends-in-waiting who walk around with an aura around them, a force field of will. On the foothills of Olympus, they can almost touch greatness. Then there are the rest, who'll battle hard but know realistically they're not going to win or get anywhere near a medal. It's this faction who have their eyes on stalks, taking everything in, soaking up the experience.

Inside the walls, the Village transforms from prison to free holiday camp. Everything is pristine and fresh looking, a bit like walking onto the Wisteria Lane set of *Desperate Housewives*. The grass is perfectly manicured; road and pavement surfaces glass smooth. To complete the perfect town there are post offices (your address for the two weeks: First name, Surname, Sport, The Olympic Village, Athens – but after you've checked the post office once and not received anything the novelty rather wears off), town squares, pool halls, cinemas, hair dressers, manicurists, boutiques filled with cuddly toy mascots, and fridges of Powerade and chillers full of ice creams at every turn. All the shops are shiny new and run by ever-smiling attendants. It's too perfect. As one athlete says, 'The first time you walk in is the most striking. You go into this place and you realise that it's built to be a town afterwards where people are going to live their lives. You're slightly overwhelmed at how organised it is.'

The Athens Village was built to hold 16,000 athletes and officials, so not everyone in the Village is a freaky eight foot tall giant. Most of Team GB's 32-strong HQ sport support staff were based there, the majority of whom were average height, average build. Here's an extract from the matter-of-fact BOA briefing note about Village life:

> Everyone will be sharing a twin bedded room. Baths, showers, toilets and wash basins provided on a ratio of one to four occupants. Shopping, laundry and other services will be available as well as a wide range of leisure and recreational activities.

A rather clinical description of a lot of fun.

Living the life of a mayfly in reverse, for just one month of its existence the Olympic Village actually operates as a beautiful Olympic Village. After its brief moment in the spotlight it becomes a housing estate and, like most Olympians, vanishes to suburban anonymity. In our Village there was an amphitheatre where the Village mayor and delegates from the Olympic Committee formally welcomed each team as they arrived, raising their national flag and (badly) singing each national anthem. I hope the amphitheatre is getting some good use, perhaps a setting for open-air theatre and concerts in the warmth of the Mediterranean evening. I very much suspect the worst.

Each Olympic Village has its own unique flavour, imbued by the host nation and its particular moment in history.

Susie Murphy remembers Mexico back in '68. 'The Mexico Village was very "happy happy", all guitars and Mexican music. It felt far off and exotic. The Village was just amazing. It was a village in every sense of the word – the shops, the restaurants. We [fencers] were sharing with the women rowers. We were all in one little apartment, all scrunched up together. They had this block for the women, separate from the men. Although some got through somehow, some slipped the net,' she laughed.

Four years later, Susie remembers Munich being totally different, 'It was very Germanic and well organised. A very, very good Village. Munich was different because we each had our own rooms, which was fab. Every (female) athlete had an en suite which was unheard of. It was very well organised. It had these lovely discotheques and shops'.

Later in the '70s, as the discipline of sports science began to emerge, Montreal proudly hosted a mobile physiology lab, although it was used more for interest and amusement rather than for actual science, being too close to competition for the information to be of any use. Nick Bell remembered excitedly, 'All the fencers went along to do all the VO_2 max stuff which is much more common nowadays. And we [the fencers] came out the same as Brendan Foster and the swimmers for cardiovascular fitness. We were really fit. Fencing is a really understated sport but when you think about it, it is very physical. Our leg strengths were way up with the rowers – you're constantly lunging – so we were quite chuffed'.

Los Angeles, the home of Hollywood and surf culture, had a movie theatre showing *Indiana Jones and the Raiders of the Lost Ark* and the Beach Boys playing an open-air concert. Moving on to 1988, the South Korean Village resonated with the beginnings of sky-high growth in Asian economies. Steve Batchelor remembers, 'In Seoul, the Village was made up of these cramped tower blocks, which were really squeezed together. You could almost chat to the guys in the next block from your window. You could certainly shout a conversation with the next tower'.

In Atlanta, the Village was in a university and, according to one resident, was 'pretty low scale compared to Sydney and Barcelona which were built specially'. Still, it wasn't a complete loss. As video-games became more sophisticated and mainstream in the '90s, the video-game arcade got a lot of use (too much use as some Olympians' sprained thumbs and bleary eyes attested). Four years on, a first-time Olympian's impression of the Sydney Village rang true with the national stereotype.

'I remember walking in for the first time. There was quite a lot of excitement in our group. We walked up the road and there was a barbecue just happening in the middle of the street. You could just ask for anything and no money changed hands. It's a really surreal experience.'

Most recently, in Beijing, the Chinese authorities tried to make up for the reports of forced clearances of Beijing slums to make way for Olympic infrastructure by injecting the Village with culture. One Beijing Olympian told me, 'They had an opera or a play on every night in the little theatre in the middle [of the Village] where you could go and relax. The accommodation in Beijing was good. It was actually nice.' He sounded quite surprised. The Chinese authorities weren't exactly laissez faire though, with gambling strictly banned, only 'family friendly' DVDs in the Village shops and alcohol not allowed anywhere in the Village, making it difficult to break the Team GB no alcohol, no smoking code of conduct.

Everywhere, everything is dangerously free. Having learnt that you pay for things for the first 25 years or so of your life, suddenly not paying for stuff does feel strange. The effect of everything being free is treacherously addictive and, even despite the warnings from team managers, athletes get over-excited. One Beijing gold medallist sums it up, 'It's just crazy, it takes your breath away a little bit. Free stuff for two weeks!'

The Sydney Olympian's experience was the same. 'After the barbecue, we went into one of the coffee shops, which had trolleys full of stuff and you could just order coffee after coffee after coffee, all free, and you're like "How's this working?" But you have to try and keep a lid on it all until you've finished competing.'

'Free' is most dangerous in the food hall where you have infinite choice, unlimited 24/7 access and no cost. The BOA prepared us for the immensity of the dining hall with a mastery of understatement: 'Dining facilities will cater for a broad range of international cultures, tastes and nutritional needs.'

While the rest of the Village is very nice and exciting, it is, in essence, a high-security housing estate with lots of free entertainment, temporarily populated by freaks and physiotherapists. The food hall is a different matter. You don't see one of these anywhere else on the planet. Afterwards, while the Village easily transforms into a housing estate, the food hall is so unique it is surplus to requirements. Steve Batchelor went back to look at the Barcelona food hall a few years ago. It's a huge multi-storey car park.

Back in 1992 it was quite different. 'In Barcelona, the food hall could hold 3,500 people at one sitting. They did food for every nationality in the world. And it was open 24/7, catering for the swimmers going off at four in the morning or people coming back really late at night from an event.'

While today we can all pop out for a Vietnamese, Italian or French meal, or order a Chinese, Thai, Malaysian or Indian takeaway from the comfort of our sofa at home, just a decade or two ago access to a range of international cuisine was a rare occurrence. An American gold medallist and resident of the Los Angeles Village reminded me, 'It was a novelty to have all those different foods presented to you. Now it's standard operating procedure, but back then it was pretty cool. You could order anything you wanted at any time of day!'

While there is every food imaginable, part of the food hall is comfortably familiar to almost all the Olympians. Here's a fellow Athens Olympian: 'You walk in and the first thing you see is a McDonald's on your right.' Shockingly to most Olympians, McDonald's is busy from the first day, when everyone is still competing. I sat across the table from a mountainous Eastern European woman shot-putter and watched astonished as she grazed her way across a crescent of half a dozen McDonald's Big Macs. I was even more astonished when I saw her toddle into the Olympic stadium to compete two days later.

Hockey man Steve Batchelor also saw some serious eating. 'In Barcelona we had three days between matches and we probably weren't quite so serious because we weren't such a good team. So one evening we had a pizza eating competition at the Village pizza place. We had some big lads, one farmer, a guy called Rob Hill, who could really put it away. We had stacks and stacks of pizzas, just eating as much as we could.' Steve didn't go crazy himself, he'd learnt his lesson in Los Angeles.

'My nickname in '84 was Batchburger, it's still on my stick bag which one of my kids is using. The food hall was just open all the time and I used to go and eat loads of crap. Nobody really controlled it. So I started putting on weight. Eventually the manager brought in scales and they weighed us every morning to make sure we were keeping a constant weight.'

More exciting than the range of food, the food hall gives you the opportunity to eat next to some really, really famous people. Granted, in the Village you're constantly surrounded by the world's best athletes, but some are a lot more famous than others. And the famous ones are without their normal huge teams of minders, security guards and lackeys.

Batchburger continues, 'There are times when you sit down [in the food hall] and you've got Boris Becker sitting next to you. And nobody bothers him. You don't start going autograph hunting'.

Nick Bell remembers bumping into the likes of Princess Anne and Seb Coe at his Olympics in Montreal and LA but managed to resist asking for autographs. 'For once you are on an equal footing. It's your five minutes of glory and you don't want to devalue it by being star struck.'

You're all equals in the Village.

A megastar moment can happen when you're least expecting it. You might find Rafael Nadal in the laundry unadvisedly mixing his whites and colours, as Bradley Wiggins did in Beijing, or have a famous sprinter flirt with you on the way there.

A 21-year-old blonde Brit at her first Olympics in Sydney remembered, 'I was just walking to the end of the street to get to the laundry room and these three guys stopped me.' Grinning at her they demanded a toll for her to pass. 'They were just joshing and clearly wanted an excuse to stop me and talk. We were standing outside a block with a Mexican flag so I asked joking whether they were Mexican?'

The response, 'No I'm from Namibia. Hi, I'm Frankie, Frankie Fredericks.'

She concluded, 'One minute you're a nobody walking down the street and then you bump in to these people who you've seen on TV and you're flirting with them.'

Sadly for them, a few megastar Olympians are just too famous to resist and can't live effectively in the Village. A Barcelona Olympian told me, 'The only ones who were pestered were the Dream Team. They weren't staying in the Village, being multi-multi millionaires, but when they visited they were mobbed, big time, not by the English, but by the Russians and the Eastern Bloc countries'.

In Sydney, Roger Federer stayed in the Olympic Village. By Beijing his fame was such he opted for a hotel to avoid other athletes chasing him for his photograph. The Williams sisters also avoided the Village in Beijing. Lionel Messi and his Argentine football team only stayed in the

Village briefly, before moving to a private hotel (reportedly because there wasn't internet access and TV in the rooms), leaving the Brazilian footballers to tough it out in the Village, where gaggles of other athletes followed them around, Ronaldinho in particular.

A large contingent of non-megastar Olympians stay out of the Village before and during competition, not because they're hounded for autographs, but out of pure convenience. The sailors, rowers, canoeists and equestrian athletes all stayed outside the Village in Beijing because of the distance of their venues from the city. The British triathlon team stayed in rented houses in Sydney before their competition, not for convenience but in an attempt to help their psychological preparation. Sian Brice remembers how it didn't work. 'We did this strange thing of staying in these houses, not in the Village, but not being guided very well. The three of us were quite disparate as a group and I did get quite nervous. That is the just the way it goes. I would have coped better in the Village.'

Tom James and his GB rowing teammates stayed out near the rowing course for both Athens and Beijing, but Team GB tried to keep them involved in the Olympic spirit.

'In Beijing, when we got to the hotel we were staying at in Shunyi [an hour and a half out of the city near the rowing lake] we each had a message, a directive from the team management of the BOA. It just seemed so stupid at the time: "We kindly ask that athletes wear their red shirts on Mondays, white shirts on Tuesdays and blue shirts Wednesdays" in this sort of rotating pattern. I just thought, what a load of rubbish, I've got more important things to think about than what colour kit I'm wearing each day. And I hadn't even brought most of my red stuff, I remember looking through my bags to find lots of white and blue. But anyway it came round to dinner time and suddenly in the back of your head you're thinking, well everyone else is probably going to be wearing red, so my roommate and I put on our red things, feeling a bit self-conscious and wondering whether everyone else was going to do it. Anyway, it was awesome. You go down to the hotel lobby and there are red shirts everywhere. We had the canoeists, physios, rowers, a good 150 people. It was just a sea of red shirts. It struck me very powerfully that while it was a very simple request, you know that all the other athletes, whether in the Olympic Village or out at the sailing or wherever, are wearing red shirts. It was quite uplifting. Everyone is buying into this one little ask. It was very important actually because it meant that those people in the room cared about what they were doing. Everyone had done this one simple thing but the impression of being "Team GB" was quite powerful. There was a definite feeling that we were a better-organised team and better looked after than all the other nations there.'

Team GB's inclusive approach to create one team, wherever they happened to be staying in China, clearly worked and contributed to their best performance for 100 years.

The Crufts of humanity

The best thing about the Village, even better than the famous people, food and free stuff is the amazing variety of humankind. Pick a corner in the shade and sit and watch for half an hour. It's like going on a human safari or to the Crufts of all mankind: all colours, shapes and creeds. The contrast emphasises the wonderful diversity of the human race. Watch a basketball game and everyone's tall – so no one looks it. In the Village you might get a 14-year-old Russian gymnast sitting between a 130kg Turkish weightlifter and a seven-foot Chinese basketball player.

Play guess-the-sport (shaven legs and tiny little T-Rex arms – cyclists; heaviest makeup – synchronised swimmers) and take your Olympic manual to tick off the rarer or more beautiful species. Swedish sailing team – tick. French volleyball player – tick. Cuban heavyweight boxer – tick.

British rower, Josh West, is 6'10". That is so tall that he is constantly told in astonished tones, 'You're very tall!' by passing strangers. It's quite amusing to watch from the sidelines but after the first 5,000 or so such comments it must get rather draining. But Josh manages to give a polite smile and a gentle shrug. A shy man for many years, he often wore his height as a burden, slightly stooped. Today, after two Olympics and the silver medal in Beijing, he's grown into his height. He stands proud and tall, no longer seemingly slightly apologetic for his size. In the Olympic Village Josh realised he wasn't that tall after all.

'First I met a German man who was a clear foot taller than me. Then I met Yao Ming, the Chinese basketball player (and an icon of the Beijing Games) who was literally a foot and a half taller than me. And I stood eye-to-eye with a Russian volleyball player – from the ladies' team. But then again, I stood in a security queue behind Kobe Bryant, who plays for the LA Lakers, and was taken aback by how small he was.' It's all relative, Josh.

Yao Ming stood out like a lighthouse in the Sydney Olympic Village too. Bas van de Goor, who played on the Dutch volleyball team in Atlanta and Sydney (winning gold in Atlanta alongside his younger brother), remembered walking into the food hall in Sydney with his team at the same time as another big man 100m away. Bas is 6'10" – he's been called the Michael Jordan of volleyball. His team averaged 6'6".

'Our whole team were looking at this guy because it looked like he was standing on something. When he got close enough I saw it was Yao Ming. At 7'6" he was impressive. He was looking for someone and passed us like we were invisible. I thought I saw him smile and could almost hear him thinking, "Those guys thought they were big."'

Nick Bell was also struck by the giants. 'The most unusual shape were the basketball players. Never seen anything like them. Some of them so tall but can't have been good athletes. Just like human trees.'

Steve Batchelor thinks the best bit about the Village is seeing all the guys from other sports. 'The weird, the large, the strange. You might get a gymnast and on the TV you think they're quite big but you see them next to you, and you realise they're midgets. Little power-houses. One night Sean Curley and I were in the supper queue in the food hall and Sean starts chatting in sign language to a Chinese girl basketball player. Seven foot something. Unbelievable. She was a monster. Sean was putting his hands up against hers and she was loving it. She was huge."

I had a similar experience with two seven foot Chinese women's volleyball players. Back in their villages at home no doubt they feel like freaks. But here in the Olympic Village, they're at home. Seven foot is commonplace. Freaks are normal. Normal is freakish.

For Susie Murphy, the width of some athletes was more shocking: 'It was the field athletes. The discus throwers with one huge arm. The women particularly; the guys you expect to be big and bulked up but the women looked just as big. The other [shocking] ones were the weightlifters and the Greco-Roman wrestlers from Iran and Eastern Europe. They were quite small but really bulked up and their legs are just so wide, because that's what they use to lift the other wrestler or the weights.' Another Olympian was also most struck by the weightlifters, labelling them 'extraordinary midgets'.

You walk into the Village expecting giants but in the full spectrum of sizes and shapes there are even normal people. In fact, it's quite surprising how many athletes there are who are nondescript, average height and build. Maybe they're all the physiotherapists. A Sydney Olympian shared my surprise, 'I think you do realise that being an athlete doesn't mean you have to be a certain physique or makeup. That you could be ridiculously tall and skinny or you could be short and quite fat. We were like, what sport's that?'

Playing human safari, spotting the most unusual shapes and sizes, is a good way of killing time in the Village. When you've been warned off the excitement of the games room and banned from grazing in the food hall, time can start to drag.

An American Olympian felt the frustration. 'It [the Village] got more tedious than fun to be honest. It was so far from the competition venue there was only time for one training session each day so you had a long time to sit on your hands waiting for the next practice. You hang around and stay out of the sun and try not to make eye contact with your opponents.'

This leaves plenty of time for another favourite Village pastime. Spot the hottie. After all, the Village caters for all tastes. One female Olympian raved about the boxers who would skip outside her block in Barcelona to get down to weight before their fights, sweat dripping over chiselled torsos.

Another Barcelona veteran went misty-eyed on the subject, clearly still able to picture the scenes in his mind's eye. 'Some of the bodies on some of the girls were unbelievable. I mean we were an amateur sport really when we played. But some of these top athletes close up. The bodies. Unbelievable. Unbelievable.'

Finishing touches

Athens
Thursday 12 August 2004
In the summer heat and breezeless swelter of the training area the sweat beads and runs along our skin, dropping into small puddles and splashes on the floor beneath. I like it – recognition of our work. I find myself relishing my strength and fitness that I've worked so many years to build. I will only be weaker from this day forward. Quite a morose thought.

The last training session concluded, we shower and change and go and wait for the rest of the squad. Team manager's instructions: must be another team briefing before we get the coach back. I pull a couple of chilled Powerades from one of the many fully stacked fridges, toss one to Jamie and we sit in the sunshine on one of the newly manicured lawns with one of the women's tream.

We've barely sat down when one of the Oakley reps approaches us again and foists more free sunglasses upon us from his huge kit bag. We only take a couple of pairs each today – another £300-worth on eBay. It's getting ridiculous. Our lady teammate takes another pair of M-Frames just to use as a hair band until she gets back to her room.

Adidas and Nike sunglasses reps are also wandering around, trying to make friends with the athletes – sunglasses are one of few bits of kit which are more or less left to the athletes' discretion as they're deemed a personal, technical choice. No large logos are allowed of course (tiny Nike ticks or Adidas stripes are OK) but getting your latest range of sunglasses in the 100m final or the cycling road race is exposure worth tens of millions of dollars for Oakley and the rest.

Olympians of all nations come and go, all the athletes radiating confidence. It's all one big poker game, but only a few really have a potentially winning hand. Eastern Europeans pass in their loud and garish shell suits. The Chinese team is shepherded along by its minders, all perfectly matching with tracksuit tops all zipped up to the regulation extent. The Italians are favoured for one of the disciplines and don't they just know it as they pose and strut. Once their training is complete they whip off their tops to bask in the sunshine and reveal their chiselled mahogany torsos. Our blonde physio shamelessly eyes the Italian Adonises.

I'm surprised at how many of the top athletes in each competition seem to be great friends with each other. Between training sessions there is much shaking of giant hands and patting on beefy shoulders, all of them with their chests puffed out like pigeons and confident game faces on. I've overheard talk about each other's weddings (one guy asking his fiercest rival for gold whether he can make it over in late September – the month that becomes Olympian wedding season by default). The cream of each team is more comradely and respectful to their peers of other nations than they are to junior members of their own teams. Presumably the elite can relate better to each other but it's surprising and, I'm embarrassed to recognise, slightly hurtful to a man lower down the ranks. I thought I'd finally made it – but now I see there's another club I haven't been invited to join yet.

One by one our whole squad congregates, chatting about the conditions and who looks good in training, but you can sense we're all keen to get back to our rooms and escape the suffocation of the Olympic competition venue. After another ten minutes we're just about to give up on the team manager and walk en masse to the coach when he finally arrives, looking a little flustered. I see the man to his left and I understand why. There's the famous Cheshire cat smile.

The Prime Minister Tony Blair and his wife Cherie approach grinning, flanked by serious looking men in dark glasses and suits who must be sweating buckets. They've got ear comms pieces, just like in 24. Ah, now I understand the suits – hiding the guns.

Cherie is the most amazing flirt, 'Tony, Tony, get a photo of me and all these hulking men'. She whisks a small camera from her bag which she presses into his hands. Weird to hear Tony's first name used not in some smarmy PR, spin doctor way, but in a genuine husband and wife type way.

Tony fumbles with the little digital camera, while Cherie nestles amongst us. After another few moments of ineffectual fiddling, Cherie loses patience and Tony is ordered to hand over the camera to a security guy and to get in the photo. Hilarious to see one of the most powerful men in the world being henpecked. It's crystal clear who wears the trousers. Tony obediently obeys and slots in amongst us, visibly relieved to be on the other side of the camera.

'Cheese!'

There's the famous smile again.

As the red eye flash counts down to the picture, Rob, one of our guys standing in the back row, grabs Nick's shorts and in one smooth movement tries to whip them down. Cat-like, Nick moves like lightning to grab hold of his pockets before he's exposed from the waist down in a photo with the smiling PM and his wife.

'Robert, I'd like to leave my shorts on thanks,' Nick is not amused.

Princess Anne had been rather more demure when she visited us at the training centre a few days earlier. We were in our ice jackets cooling off and lowering our core temperatures which provided a good thread for conversation, avoiding the normal awkward pleasantries. Turns out, after equestrian events the horses are cooled off under icy showers. I'm not sure how I feel about being compared to a horse. Once on to the safe ground of horses the Princess doesn't stop talking. Nice seeing such a passion.

We don't get on to horses with the Blairs. After some polite chat about how we're feeling about our events they leave with the last words, 'We are all behind you.' We smile and say gracious thank yous but fear grips my stomach. It's easy to forget, lost in training or behind the safe walls of the Village, that the eyes of the world are turning to watch us.

Finally we get back on the bus. More damn time to think.

the doping arms race

Athens
Friday 13 August 2004

It's everywhere this morning – the first big drugs story of the Games. Every TV channel, every newspaper. I suppose it was inevitable but I didn't think it would be so early: the day of the opening ceremony itself.

Last night Kostas Kenteris, the 200m sprinter and Greek national hero, was called for a drugs test, along with his training partner Katerina Thanou (who herself got silver in the 100m at Sydney). But they couldn't be found in the Village. Apparently no one knew where the two most high profile athletes in Greece were.

Later, in the early hours of this morning and having missed the test window, the two of them were involved in a motorbike crash and are now in hospital with light injuries. The IOC President, Jacques Rogge himself, has announced he's created a disciplinary committee to investigate.

Riding a motorbike? I cannot begin to imagine our head coach or team manager's reaction if after training I jumped on a Suzuki and revved it up with my girlfriend on the back. They'd implode and drop me on the spot.

Who's going to light the Olympic cauldron in tonight's opening ceremony now?

On my way to training all the Greeks I meet are looking touchingly heart-broken. The police, the security guys outside the training venue, the volunteers in their cheery colourful shirts – they all look downcast. The TV clips of women crying in the streets weren't exaggerating the national feeling. And Kenteris's face is on billboards all over the city which just rubs in the pain.

A few athletes poke fun at the Greeks naivety, 'He was the only white guy in the 200m final in Sydney. Wasn't it obvious?'

Looking at my opposition out training I'm surprised at how disconcerted I feel. Are any of them taking something extra while I spend my life tired and broken and trying desperately to measure up?

Cheat a little or cheat a lot?

At some point in each modern Olympics a variation on the Kenteris story breaks. The question for the athlete is not if but when it will happen, and who'll be caught. Will it be one of your rivals? Will your Olympic final be forever mired in doping controversy?

Will it be you?

No one likes being tested – clean or doper. Firstly, there is the personal awkwardness of having to piss into a pot with a middle-aged man eyeing your tackle like a hawk at close range. But infinitely worse than that degradation is the sweating over the potential of a false positive; a spiked sample, a lab switch or an innocent protein supplement that has minute traces of nandrolone or another nasty. And that's if you're clean. I don't know how dopers deal with the stress. Perhaps they take drugs for that too.

A bit of a dull confession – I never once took performance-enhancing drugs and I never saw any being taken. I experimented with creatine for a season, a supplement meant to help build muscle mass, but it wasn't for me. Sure, I drank protein shakes by the gallon, took various vitamin supplements (mainly vitamin C and zinc) to help bolster my immune system, popped legal anti-inflammatory and painkilling drugs when injured or aching badly, which was pretty much all the time, and drank a lot of coffee – but that was because I liked coffee, not for the caffeine stimulus. Sorry if that's a little unexciting but it sets my views in context.

Another anti-climactic confession: I was never ever offered doping products. Would I have taken them if they were offered to me? I like to think not. I was fighting tooth and nail every day against my squad mates for selection. I knew how hard we all worked, how much we'd sacrificed and how much each of us wanted Olympic glory. If I'd taken something to give me an edge of a second or two over my closest rivals then being selected over them would have been disgustingly empty. Going on to the Games and having parents and loved ones cheering from the stands, waving flags and bursting with pride, before all the adulation and general patting on the back from friends and total strangers you meet in the street – surely each pat on the back would eat away at you inside? Every cheery 'well done' would chip away another sliver of self respect – until what's left?

Maybe that's too sanctimonious. I like to think I wouldn't have taken up an offer of drugs but perhaps I could have rationalised doping. My lungs aren't as big as some. My blood isn't as thick with oxygen-carrying red blood cells as others. I was out of training more than average with injury. Doping could have just levelled the playing field? Perhaps. Thankfully I never had the opportunity for my resolve to be tested.

Doping prevalence is all about the cultural norms of each sport and the squads of athletes within. In Grand Tour cycling, doping seemed to hit epidemic proportions a few years ago. When drug taking is rife it makes it all the easier for up-and-coming athletes to justify doping to themselves. If everyone is doing it – why shouldn't I? If my heroes, the guys I've idolised for years, are on the stuff, then surely it's OK? It feels like cheating, but only a little bit. Little-white-lie cheating. Cheat-lite.

Behavioural economist Dan Ariely, in his excellent book *Predictably Irrational*, recounts an intriguing experiment which gives a neat insight into the psychology of cheating. Ariely got a group of Harvard students to take a 50 question, multiple-choice quiz, with each student receiving a small financial reward dependent on the number of right answers. First the control group was tested. On average they scored 32.6. Next, another group of these smart, competitive students was put through their paces, but this group were able to cheat and see the right answers. The average of the group that could cheat if they chose to was 36.2.

Perhaps this was down to a morally dubious minority who took advantage of the 'cheat sheet', enabling them to put in super high scores and take the most money, whilst the majority of these future leaders of America were as honest as you'd expect and resisted the temptation? When Ariely and his team looked at each student's papers in more detail this is what they found.

> Rather than finding a few bad apples weighed the averages, we discovered that the majority of people cheated, and that they cheated just a little bit.

This is why the cultural norms in a sport are so important in the fight against doping. When the culture allows doping to feel like cheating just a little bit (as per European pro-cycling in the 1990s) it's not just a few 'bad sorts' that will consider it – the majority will. Popping that first pill would almost be easy, barely any soul ache at all.

My sport was one where it would have been difficult morally to justify doping to yourself. I knew all my squad mates were clean. I didn't need to see test results. I just knew. Doping wasn't in the culture. Doping was serious cheating. It was that simple. Not little-white-lie cheating, but big time cheating, all-my-friends-in-the-team-would-have-disowned-me cheating. I also knew that our main international competitors, mostly developed Western nations, had clean squads. I couldn't be sure of each individual competitor, but I was pretty sure none of the teams had a systematic doping culture. After all, I knew many of the athletes personally and over the years had trained with quite a few of them. China was the wild card, the one squad I wasn't sure about. I knew none of their athletes and attempts at communication at competitions failed utterly. A few Eastern Europeans from smaller nations were caught for steroid abuse every other year or so.

Perhaps strangely I didn't begrudge them their drugs. Perhaps because we had so many other advantages over them (some of the best coaches in the world, full National Lottery support, international training camps, great equipment) and they just were desperate for a break. More likely it was because we didn't lose to them.

For me the most important driver behind not searching out and taking the magic pills was the resultant effect on teammates. You train and sweat and hurt with your squad for years and, whilst ultimately you vie against them for national team and Olympic selection, they become like your brothers (or sisters) in arms. The probable lack of doping by our main international competitors made drug taking less attractive but it was witnessing the daily sweat and sacrifice of our squad that made taking drugs, and thereby potentially unfairly demoting others from the Olympics, truly impossible.

Apart from the moral challenges of doping, the pragmatist in me also recognised that in my sport doping didn't automatically mean victory. Yes, steroids or blood doping might have helped but technique, tactics, psychology, team dynamics, the training programme and even luck probably contributed to overall performance to a greater degree.

In sports like sprinting or hammer throwing, which have perhaps fewer variables, doping can make a more definitive difference and is consequentially more tempting. Tempting enough, it seems, for Olympic champion Kenteris to risk international disgrace in search of Olympic immortality. The Kenteris/Thanou humiliation on the eve of the Athens Olympics was particularly high profile given their national status and the host nation's weight of expectation. Greece didn't have a plethora of other potential gold medallists to fixate on and to personalise their Olympic aspirations. It was perhaps the biggest scandal since Ben Johnson's failed test in 1988, in that most iconic and purest of Olympic races, the 100m. But the Games lost their innocence long before Johnson stared bull-like down the Seoul track with his yellowed, bloodshot eyes.

She-males, blood doping and a drunken Swede

Like many revellers of the Swinging Sixties, the Olympics had lost its virtue by the end of that decade. It was the era of soft drugs, free love and The Beatles. But it also saw the peak of the Cold War – the Cuban missile crisis, Vietnam and the erection of the Berlin Wall. It was the malign influence of global power politics, of Communist versus Capitalist, which lost the Olympics its purity. Today, with the USSR disintegrated and Capitalism largely victorious, it is apt that it is now largely the self-serving pursuit of wealth which drags the Games into the mire of doping and drives the creation of designer drugs.

Back in the 1960s though, life was simpler, as were the drugs and the drug tests. Britain's Susie Murphy was selected as a member of the foil team for the 1968 Mexico City Games, having been crowned British champion earlier that year. The youngest Olympic fencer ever, barely 18, the five foot nothing schoolgirl saw the product of the Soviet doping programme first hand.

'I remember being at the Village restaurant and I turned around and there was this huge … thing.' Susie is temporarily lost for words at how to describe the vision in front of her. 'I mean, it was a woman but it was, well, borderline.

'This was back in the Cold War, with the Iron Curtain countries. The women were huge, like these two famous Russian track and field athletes Tamara and Irena Press. They were pumping their athletes with drugs, particularly in track and field. It was very unsophisticated; they even had manly hair. It was quite clear they were on something. It became obvious they had to test and establish exactly what side of the fence we were on. I remember being tested to make sure I was female.'

Looking at the photo of the cute little schoolgirl, excited to be in her Olympic tracksuit, it seems pretty ridiculous. The IOC brought in sex and basic drug testing at the Mexico Games in response to the masculine appearance of a number of 'ladies' pumped up on anabolic steroids who had started appearing on the international athletics circuit. Most prominent were the Press sisters. In Tokyo in 1964, Tamara took gold and set Olympic records in both the discus and shot, whilst her younger sister won gold in the pentathlon. They were withdrawn from competition in 1966, before the Mexico Olympics and its sex tests. This was long before today's sophisticated testing and the sex test meant a degrading hands-on physical examination.

'Everyone had a test. I've still got my certificate,' Susie reminisces. And just in case Susie had become a man in the interim, she was tested again in Munich and Montreal, passing all three with flying colours and gaining three certificates of womanhood.

As well as being the inaugural Olympics for sex and drug testing, Mexico City was the first Olympics held in a developing country, the first in a Spanish-speaking nation and the first to feature separate teams from East and West Germany. But what pre-occupied athletes and coaches was the city's altitude. Mexico City is 7,300ft, 2,240m above sea level. No summer Games before or since has taken place at an altitude remotely as high. To acclimatise, Susie and her teammates in the explosive sport of fencing were sent out six weeks before the Games began. This was still very much in the amateur 'turn up and give it a go' era of British sport so the six week acclimatisation camp shows how seriously national teams were taking the altitude.

The lower air resistance helped new records to be set in many track and field events, including the discus, high jump and long jump. In the triple jump three different athletes collectively broke the world record five times during competition. But it was Bob Beamon's feat in the long jump that was to prove the most enduring. In the first jump of the competition the American jumped 8.90m and set a world record that would last 23 years. Beamon broke the previous record by 55cm, a vast margin. Since the turn of the century the average improvement on previous world records had been just 6cm. Imagine being the next athlete to jump.

Whilst the altitude helped the jumping and throwing athletes to new records, the endurance athletes had to struggle through their events. The Mexico City air contains the same percentage of oxygen (21 per cent) as at sea level, the reduced air pressure lowers the amount of oxygen inhaled in each breath, resulting in an effective oxygen content of about 16 per cent. For finely-tuned endurance athletes operating towards the edge of human capabilities, reducing the amount of oxygen available by 25 per cent has drastic consequences on performance. Unless, of course, you are fully acclimatised to altitude.

African distance runners, most of whom lived and trained in the highlands, exploded onto the Olympic scene at Mexico. The Kenyan men took seven medals across the 800m, 1,500m, 3,000m steeple-chase, 5,000m and 10,000m disciplines, three of them gold. The theory took hold that athletes from high altitudes had 'thicker blood', which helped them win in the thin air of Mexico. Subsequent Olympics nearer sea level have shown African distance runners to be just as formidable across altitudes but their dominant performance in Mexico focused athletes and scientists on the benefits of altitude training and the effects it has on the blood.

Being the first Olympics to test athletes for drugs, Mexico City was also inevitably the first Games at which an athlete was disqualified for doping. Ironically, given the vastly more disturbing practices that were to come, the ignominy of the first doping failure belongs to Hans-Gunnar Liljenwall, a member of the Swedish pentathlon team, who was disqualified for having alcohol in his system. Hans reportedly had 'two beers to calm his nerves' before taking part in the pistol shoot. Whilst this sounds perfectly innocent (what could be more natural than a beer to help relax?), the right dose of alcohol can reduce micro-tremor and involuntary movements of the hands, potentially improving accuracy in target sports such as archery or shooting. Was Hans 'doping', using chemical substances with the deliberate intention of altering perfor-mance, or just having a beer? Only Hans can know for sure.

In the same year, a long way from Mexico, Dr Manfred Hoeppner, East Germany's Chief Medical Officer, submitted a report to his government. It recommended the systematic administration of steroids to East German athletes. The darkest chapter in the history of doping had begun. For the following two decades the East Germans dominated their chosen sports and poisoned thousands of their own people with dangerous and transformational drugs.

Susie Murphy was selected again in 1972 for the ill-fated Munich Olympics. 'By then drug taking had got more sophisticated. Do you remember Lasse Viren and our 400m runner David Jenkins?'

The Fin, Lasse Viren, won both the 5,000m and 10,000m in Munich and took both titles again in 1976. In the Munich 5,000m he spectacularly fell just before halfway, giving the leading pack a 35m break. Viren recovered well enough not only to win but to set a new world record in the process. He is rumoured to have been the first successful practitioner of blood doping. One of his teammates (Kaario Maanika) later admitted to using the technique. The practice of 'auto-transfusion' (extracting your own blood and re-infusing it several weeks later shortly before a race to benefit from the extra oxygen carrying capacity), a type of blood doping, wasn't actually banned until 1986. Perhaps this was because of its invisible nature, being profoundly more subtle than steroid-fuelled Soviet she-males, or perhaps because of the challenges of its detection. With auto-transfusion you are only putting your own blood back in your body, there are no drugs to be detected.

In the same year as Munich, a triumvirate of scientists, Elblom, Goldbard and Gullbring, published a landmark study in the Journal of Applied Physiology showing just how potent blood doping could be. The scientists took ⅘ of a litre of blood from three men. Four weeks later they re-infused their blood back into them. In the four week window their bodies had created more red blood cells to make up for the earlier blood loss. With the old blood re-infused the men were now super-charged. Their hematocrit levels (the percentage of oxygen carrying red blood cells per volume of blood) were up an average of 13 per cent. Their maximal oxygen uptake increased 9 per cent. These statistics don't mean much to those who aren't sports physiologists or elite athletes, so how about this one: on a short sprint to exhaustion the supercharged men could run 23 per cent longer than their old selves – 23 per cent! Given Olympic medals are decided on differences of fractions of a per cent this study caused a huge stir in the world of elite sport. The genie was out of the bottle – the potential of tampering with blood was too seductive to ignore.

And Scottish runner Jenkins? Susie remembers, 'A silver medallist in Munich [in the 4 x 400m relay]. Well, he was involved heavily in drugs. He ended up being done big time.'

Susie isn't exaggerating. While he never failed a test as an athlete, years after retirement Jenkins was convicted of smuggling $70m worth of steroids into the US from Mexico. During his conviction he admitted using steroids during his athletic career. He was sentenced to seven years in jail although he only served nine months. The same year Jenkins founded the sports nutrition company Next Proteins which launched the wildly successful Designer Whey protein drinks. He remains CEO and President. Regardless of his background you can't fault his business acumen.

Susie thinks it was big business and the profit motive which drove Olympic doping in a wider sense, 'After the closing ceremony at Mexico we partied till the morning and all came home on the same chartered plane the following day, all different athletes mixed together. No prima donnas. We said our cheerios and swapped autographs. It was wonderful, all those athletes being together. Now it's different of course. Once Samaranch got all the sponsors and cameras in, the Olympics changed. It morphed into something else.'

Juan Antonio Samaranch was President of the IOC for more than twenty years, overseeing huge transformation across the 1980s and 1990s before signing off with the Sydney Olympics. A former official in Franco's regime, the Spaniard took on the leadership of a barely solvent and weak IOC, with the Olympic movement at a low ebb (Los Angeles was the only city to bid for the 1984 Games), and turned it into an immensely powerful organisation negotiating contracts worth hundreds of millions of dollars. But for some this came at the cost of the purity of the Olympic ideal and increased the attractiveness of doping, thanks to the much greater potential rewards for medallists. Susie saw the change first-hand.

'It became Olympics PLC. All the sponsors were fighting to get hold of the medallists. I saw it happening while I was competing. I was less aware of it in Mexico because I was so young. It was probably Montreal where I became conscious of it. Sponsors became really big and you had these Olympic "personalities". The reason to be was suddenly "gold or nothing". Everyone was striving for the medals because there was a lot more at stake. If you got the gold it meant that, from then on, your life had changed. It put you on a platform. That's when taking drugs became important. It gave you a chance to fast-forward up there. I believe anyone who's banned for drugs should be banned for life. There should be no way back because it's a lesson for the kids in the future. There should be no intervention by drugs at all.'

Knowing a number of clean athletes who lost out to drugs cheats – I agree with her.

EPO, The Clear and designed gold medallists

Shortly after the turn of the new millennium, early in 2000, a friend of mine shared a double bed with a pro-cyclist. He didn't sleep well. During the night the cyclist was up twice to pedal his bike on the turbo-trainer. This wasn't some maniacal training regime – this was survival. He was exercising to lift his heart rate and prevent his artificially thickened blood congealing while he slept. He was on EPO.

EPO, short for erythropoietin, is a naturally occurring hormone produced by the kidneys which stimulates the production of red blood cells (technically called erythrocytes). Artificial EPO was first produced to treat various forms of anaemia but it didn't take long for the endurance athlete community to see the potential of the compound. EPO could give you all the benefits of auto-transfusion that the Elblom, Goldbard and Gullbring study found; the greater oxygen-carrying capacity, the improved VO_2 max, the aerobic supercharging, all with a simple injection. No need to extract blood, store it hygienically and securely at the right temperature, train carefully while the body regenerates the normal levels of red blood cells before finally re-infusing. EPO injections are much simpler. And also difficult to detect – your body produces EPO naturally.

But if human beings perform much better with higher concentrations of red blood cells circulating in our system why hasn't four billion years of evolution given us all that thicker blood, with greater oxygen carrying capacity? After all, the caveman with the higher proportion of red blood cells would have, all else being equal, been able to outrun a caveman with a lower hematocrit, leaving him to be eaten by the sabre tooth tiger. Did evolution fail us?

As the premature deaths of many professional cyclists attest, the benefits of having high octane, thickened blood pumping round our system are outweighed by the greater risk of the treacle-like blood congealing (clotting) in the body and causing a stroke, heart attack or embolism. Professional athletes with their low resting pulse rates (mine hit 38 beats per minute … Thump … Thump … Thump …) are particularly at risk, the treacle having time to pause in their veins. Within four years of EPO arriving on the scene, 20 European pro cyclists had died suddenly and unexpectedly.

One athlete I spoke to mentioned EPO and the Tour de France in passing. 'EPO was endemic. But it was a level playing field. All the authorities were doing [to test for it] was testing their hematocrit. A score of over 50 was a failed test. So they would top themselves up to that level. So in a way it was a level playing field. The average age of death of a Tour de France cyclist is something like 57 because they have messed around so much with their bodies.'

While not good for overall life expectancy, EPO is wonderfully helpful for long endurance events, where continued high levels of aerobic performance are required. So it's the perfect drug for distance cycling, running or swimming, which makes it triply perfect for triathlon.

Sian Brice was Britain's top female triathlete going into the Sydney 2000 Olympics, the first Olympics to feature the sport. I asked her about the magic of EPO. Tall, slim and elegant, Brice retired after Sydney and is now a mother of two – but she's a mum that recently did an Ironman triathlon in 11 hours to celebrate her 40th birthday with a friend. Hardcore.

'Triathlon was a classic for EPO. Long distances, very aerobic and it involved cycling so it was accessible. Two days before the Sydney race they gave the top 15 of us a blood test. At that time they had started testing for artificial EPO but the test could only detect it if it was in the system in the last 48 hours so it was pretty crap.'

The benefits of EPO last up to about three weeks after the injections are stopped. Unsurprisingly no one tested positive. But Sian knew some competitors were on EPO.

'We all knew. The athletes know. In the run up to Sydney one of the girls I'd known for years went from being an outsider to a real contender. And that's in her mid-30s with all of us training our arses off. Performances can be tweaked but the closer you get to the top, the smaller the incremental changes get. But give someone EPO and it's like putting them on a bike with an engine on it.

'I spoke to a couple of her teammates. They said she was flying and was going to win the Olympics – we don't know how she's doing it. But we all knew. She improved too much. There were some classic moments in races on really hilly courses. I knew some of the girls who were at the front of the pack with her. They said they were were all out of breath and these were really fit girls, the best in the world. They looked over at her and she wasn't even breathing hard.'

Why did the woman put herself through that, why take the risks?

'There is some money in triathlon. I was getting paid. I got a car from my sponsors. We were getting $10k win bonuses for World Cups. And for her, because her home country hardly got any Olympic medals, there was a several hundred thousand Euro bonus for winning gold. It was potentially life-changing.'

Sian retired after Sydney. We may never know if Bridgette McMahon of Switzerland, who won the gold medal, was taking EPO at the time, but in 2005 she tested positive for the compound in an out-of-competition test at her home. McMahon maintains she only began taking EPO in 2005, while going through a divorce and caring for her three small children.

While EPO and other forms of blood doping had been a stalwart of the doping scene for endurance athletes for years by Sydney, there was a new drug on the block for dopers seeking explosive power. Tetrahydrogestrinone, better known as THG or 'The Clear', was the most potent designer steroid on earth when created. Just a few drops of the liquid under the tongue was an effective dose, a long way from the myriad of pills pressed upon athletes in the extensive steroid regimes of East Germany in the 1970s and '80s. The Clear was developed by a smart chemist for a San Francisco-based sports nutrition company and for several years the drug was completely undetectable. Users of The Clear sailed through every test.

The Clear was to be Sydney's doping story. Only it didn't break in Sydney. In 2003 a disgruntled sprinting coach posted a syringe with traces of THG to the US Anti-Doping Agency which allowed a test for the drug to be developed (rendering it The Unclear perhaps?). The house of cards started falling in and on 5 October 2007 American athlete Marion Jones pleaded guilty to using THG, as well as lying to a 2003 federal enquiry.

Marion Jones had taken the Sydney track and field events by storm with five medals, three of them gold. She was one of the stories of the Sydney Games; amazing athletic performance combined with feline good looks. Apart from the good looks, it was all built on sand. Four days after her admission, Jones ceded her medals to the US Olympic Committee. Later in 2007 the IOC formally stripped them from her.

For the women that medalled behind Marion, having the Olympic record books re-written several years after the event hopefully brought some emotional and psychological closure. Seeing Jones do six months in jail for lying in court about her steroid use might also have brought some spiteful pleasure, but the silver medallists behind Marion will never stand atop the podium in the Olympic stadium in front of thousands of cheering fans, see their flag lifted highest and listen to their national anthem played in honour of their triumph. No embraces with trackside parents, who'd whisper to them 'I always knew you would do it'.

One Sydney Olympic medallist who missed gold by a fraction of a second concurred, 'Having the person ahead of you disqualified doesn't take away the mental image that you've lost that race. I can't imagine if the two people in front of us were disqualified – we didn't win that race. They won whatever they might have taken.'

From a financial point of view, being announced Olympic champion almost a decade on from your Olympics is like shutting the stable door after the doped horse has bolted. Advertisers and their clients want current personalities fresh in the minds of consumers to endorse products or services. Good-looking winners with plenty of recent column inches and TV coverage. A retrospectively crowned Olympic champion, who missed the chance to get lodged in the minds of consumers during the Games is worth a fraction of what they would have been had they been seen by millions (or billions) at the podium summit. Doping athletes don't slip into their competitors' houses at night and steal their medals and tens of thousands of dollars but the effect is the same. It is surprising that you don't see more cases of silver or bronze medallists suing doped gold medallists, and the drug developers and suppliers, for damages and loss of earnings.

In 2009 the International Olympic Committee decided to re-allocate medals in three of Marion Jones' Sydney events, the 100m, 200m and long jump. Instantly they hit a problem. In the 100m, the Greek Katerina Thanou had won silver but since gone on to uproar in Athens with the motorbike crash and missed tests. The IOC decided to upgrade the third and fourth placed Jamaican duo Tayna Lawrence and Merlene Ottey to silver and bronze, leaving Katerina with her silver.

This leaves the Sydney Olympics women's 100m without a winner. That feels depressingly apt.

I've focused on steroids and blood doping (through EPO and auto-transfusion) which make you stronger and fitter respectively, but there are plenty of other drugs used in plenty of other sports. From human growth hormone and testosterone, to ecstasy-like stimulants and diuretics which help you lose weight and clear other illicit substances from the system. Even less visibly aggressive pastimes like golf, archery and concert violin playing can be tainted by beta blockers. Normally prescribed for heart problems, beta blockers lower heart rate and suppress adrenalin production, reducing tremor and allowing for a steadier shot. That said, drug use is inevitably more prevalent in the relatively one-dimensional tests of speed or strength, like the 100m or the shot put, where drugs make a bigger difference than in sports with more variables and complexity. Take hockey. Here's gold medallist Steve Batchelor's response when I asked him about drug use in his sport.

'Drugs to last a match? It didn't cross our minds really. Hockey's all about moving the ball around and stick work. Drugs won't help you with that; they'll make it worse. It's about talent.'

In theory, in sports like fencing, table tennis or football the stimulant ephedrine (similar to caffeine) can help lower reaction times and increase speed (and also lower appetite) but the benefits seem questionable. Olympic fencer and Doctor Nick Bell, 'There isn't much drugs in fencing because the gains aren't there. It's not the 100m. Having said that, the Italian favourite was caught with ephedrine in his wee before the Beijing Olympics so he didn't go. But a lot of people think it was a vendetta actually. Other people wanted him out of the team for whatever reason and he was spiked. It was all a bit of a rum do.'

There is no doubt the doping arms race will continue. As to how the shady war will play out, the Olympians I know are split pretty evenly into optimistic and pessimistic camps. One pessimist's comment sums up their argument.

'For every lab out there testing cheats, there are two researching new drugs to stay ahead of the testers.'

Triathlete Sian Brice is slightly more optimistic, 'I think the Beijing [Olympic] triathlon was clean. One of Brett Sutton's girls won. It wasn't a surprise. It's those people who come out of the woodwork, win and then never do that well again. Then it's a bit obvious.'

The athlete I talked to about the Tour de France also fell in the optimist camp.

'The Tour is getting better, I think, with the advancement of EPO testing and new teams like Sky coming in who don't have the history. I think so many of them were getting caught. In France they take it very seriously and get the police involved. It's not just a case of WADA turning up at your door and a bit in the papers. I do think they are trying to clean up their act and I think that was exemplified this Tour with different people winning every stage. You couldn't physically win day after day in the mountains without some kind of drugs. Whereas now people have good days and bad days. All will be revealed in 20–30 years' time when we can do retrospective tests.'

It will undeniably take decades to find out how we are faring today in the war against doping, as the testing technology gradually catches up with the dopers and their frozen urine and blood samples. How many other 'Clears' are being used today? Was The Clear Mk. 2 in use in Beijing? If by Rio in 2016 some of Beijing's 100m medallists haven't been stripped of their medals we should breathe a partial sigh of relief.

I'll wager the next chapter in the doping saga will see designer drugs replaced by designer Olympians. The field of genetics, which overall will hugely benefit the human race, has advanced rapidly in the 60 years or so since Cambridge scientists Watson and Crick walked into their local pub and announced they'd found the secret of life, having identified the double helix of DNA.

The genetic testing of human embryos began in the 1990s, initially to determine the sex of a potential child. Genetic testing has since expanded to be able to screen for an ever-widening range of genetically driven diseases and predispositions. In 2009 a US fertility clinic offered parents the chance to select the eye and hair colour of their baby, which would have made so called 'designer babies' a reality. While the clinic rapidly withdrew the offer, with the science of genetics continuing to advance and the cost of genome sequencing falling fast, it won't be long until some parents are selecting embryos based on preferences for height, eye colour, hair colour and even IQ range. After that it is it a matter of time until a dictatorship desperate for propaganda and international recognition, like Zimbabwe or North Korea, decides to design Olympic gold medallists. Scientists will select embryos tailored to the particular demands of targeted sports or even insert specific genes using virus hosts, to produce athletes with the genes which give the right height and arm span, the perfect balance of fast and slow twitch muscle fibre, the predisposition to develop the appropriate musculature and maximise hematocrit count. If the regime wanted a swimming gold medallist or two, no doubt the scientists would attempt to select for the genes creating a man of around 6'5", with the super long arms, the giant hands of Michael Phelps and the size 17 feet of Ian Thorpe. Perhaps they'll even be able to select for the genetic mutations which produce webbed toes? With no illicit compound for drug tests to pick up on, genetically selected athletes will be difficult to detect. Good luck WADA.

Doping is unpleasant. Not just the actual cheats, who steal money and winning memories from the more deserving. Dope testing is unpleasant. No one likes having their genitalia stared at by a random middle-aged man or woman first thing in the morning, whilst trying to squeeze a drop and all because others cheat. The potential of doping allows uncharitable rumours and suspicion to flare across the Olympics. You hear stories of needles in changing rooms. If doping was more under control you might be able to believe they are for treatment of diabetes. The greats are always suspected. Those who show sudden jumps in form even more so. Have they just sorted their technique? Or is it drugs? The athlete with a bout of acne and a temper problem – is it the steroids or does he just suffer from greasy skin and a short fuse? Whole teams that rise from nothing are always under the spotlight. Before Beijing I heard a rumour that a 30-strong Chinese squad had pulled out of a major World Cup competition the year before the Games, citing a big bout of flu, when the organisers announced they would be blood testing rather than just urine testing. The rumour was false, they turned up.

With the stakes high and getting higher as Olympic endorsements rise in value, the doping arms race will continue. The risks of being caught doping have got to be penal and the sentences draconian. A two-year ban is pointless. The biggest thing stopping athletes doping is their inner moral compass. Once they've shown that moral compass to be fallible, they're not athletes. They are thieves. Maybe they should bring back the ancient Olympic penalties of flogging and the practice of erecting statues en route to the Olympic stadium funded by the fines imposed on cheats, shaming the family name for eternity. With tougher sentencing, ever more rigorous out-of-competition testing and retrospective checks on frozen blood and urine samples, doping will, I think, eventually be brought under control.

In 10 to 20 years I will be reasonably certain whether the men I lined up against were clean or not. Until there is proof otherwise, to me they are clean. I hope they afford me the same benefit of the doubt.

lift off

The greatest shows on earth

Finally, after all the waiting, all the hype and the expense, the Olympics begin with an almighty bang. Beijing was launched with 29,000 fireworks, 10,000 performers, 80 world leaders and 200 teams of athletes in front of 90,000 fans, 100,000 police and security officials, and a billion people watching worldwide.

Olympic opening ceremonies are truly the greatest shows on earth and far better than their closing ceremony twins. The athletes and organisers are full of energy and hope rather than relief or regret. The fans are only at the start of their long-awaited holidays, with stratospheric expectations for the coming fortnight and a mutually congratulatory smugness at having got tickets for the opening ceremony. And no one is hung-over just yet.

They are the greatest shows on earth with one major caveat: 90 per cent of the four-hour marathon is dull or weird. Or both. The 10 per cent brimming with hope, expectation and spectacle makes up for the rest. There is a set formula for the ceremony in the IOC's Olympic Charter. The host country's Head of State is received by the President of the IOC and the Chair of the Organising Committee (for London 2012, the triumvirate of the Queen, Jacques Rogge and Seb Coe). Every public utterance is made three times, in French, English and the language of the host nation language, lending a stiltedness to proceedings.

So far, so unexciting.

The mad, artistic interlude begins, with each host nation keen to demonstrate its culture and depth through the medium of poetry, dancing and music. The bizarreness can be captivating. In Athens eyebrows were raised as Eros flew over pairs of frolicking lovers, while in Beijing the massed drumming hypnotised the crowd.

Then the teams of athletes parade into the stadium in the alphabetical order of the host country, apart from Greece which enters first (in all but the Athens Games) and the host nation which joins last. The parade makes up the bulk of the ceremony and as a viewer this part drags on endlessly. There are just too many athletes walking slowly in a circle and waving. Occasionally, every 50 teams or so, the parade marks a major political and historical event. In 2004, the crowd rapturously welcomed the beaming Iraqi team and the contingent from Afghanistan, which included female team members for the first time. During Sydney, Afghanistan had been under Taliban rule and was banned from competing. North and South Korea marched together as one in Athens. Sadly, by Beijing they were marching separately again. Whole new countries emerge for the first time. The flags of East Timor and Kiribati had their Olympic debuts in Athens, while recently deceased countries are noted by the commentators. Goodbye Yugoslavia, hello Serbia and Montenegro.

Like the Eurovision song contest, political differences and allegiances both large and small are amusingly displayed to the whole world. In Greece, the crowd was notably quiet as Turkey and Israel paraded but was loving and cheery as Cyprus and Portugal entered, the Greek football team's win only weeks before in Portugal's Euro 2004 football tournament fresh in the national consciousness. Djibouti's lonely marcher also got a good reception (at least Djibouti had it easy in the politics of flag bearer selection). By the end, whilst bored, you're reminded of the wonderful diversity of the people of the world and are reeling for an atlas (Kiribati – a nation of Pacific islands; Djibouti – North East Africa adjacent to Somalia; East Timor – half of a South East Asian island surrounded by the Indonesian archipelago).

The stupefied crowd are then hit by speeches from the Chair of the Organising Committee and the President of the IOC, before finally the Head of State declares the Games open. The Olympic flag is raised; the Olympic torch is passed between darlings of the host nation before ceremoniously lighting the Olympic cauldron. The world explodes with fireworks and music. No one remembers the speeches but everybody is primevally transfixed by the emotion and the flames and the athletes staring wistfully into them.

That's the viewer's perspective. In contrast, while ticket-holding fans give thanks like they've each won a golden ticket to Willy Wonka's chocolate factory, the athletes are deeply paranoid about even attending the opening ceremony. I watched with my squad mates on a little TV miles from the stadium, sitting on Team GB beanbags, waving mini-Union Jacks and cheering as our physio and psychologist marched in our place. The BOA line was that all athletes who wished to march would be able to do so but they strongly discouraged any competing in the two days following the ceremony to take part. It meant leaving the Olympic Village at 5pm, before the ceremony started at 9pm and not returning until the early hours after the finale at midnight. In reality the coaches made it clear we weren't marching whatever our preference, not that we would have done even if we'd had the option. Like us, the British track and field athletes in 2012 will also miss out on the opening ceremony, the UK athletics coach rationalising, 'They would not go shopping for eight hours before their biggest event so why would you be on your feet for that long?' Thankfully I managed to find a few rare Olympians who have actually marched.

An American gold medallist's recollection of Los Angeles: 'There's nothing like it, going through that tunnel. It's a pretty amazing experience. I'm glad we did it. As it turned out it wasn't as tiring as everyone says and no one got sick. Although maybe it would have been a different story had we not won. You hear all the horror stories about athletes getting sick or having a bad race the next day and all. It was really a once in a lifetime experience.'

It's easy to forget that most of the competitors are not from stadium-based sports. Here's a Beijing Olympian: 'I remember being totally stunned at what it's like to be on the floor of a big stadium when it's absolutely packed with people and there's a huge amount of energy focused on you. Coming from an outdoor sport you never have that perspective. It's pretty intense.'

A Sydney Olympian echoed him, 'I totally wasn't prepared for the excitement of walking in and just the flash photography going off and everything, because we never compete in stadiums so we never get that experience.'

While they wait to be called into the stadium the athletes miss much of the artistic frippery and speeches and, depending where their team is in the alphabet, much of the athletes' march. Officials try to choreograph their entry but with the excitement and the alpha personalities of most of the athletes, it's like herding over-energetic cats.

An English Los Angeles Olympian remembered, 'We were waiting in a huge field outside in '84 in teams of 700 or so strong with a big banner for each country. It was quite hot. We were all told to take our sunglasses off and were marshalled strictly by height order, but as soon as we went in we were all trying to get onto the outside lane to be seen. Watching a repeat in the Village after, I'm the only one in the outside lane with sunglasses still on. A long day but very memorable.'

A Sydney athlete also remembers the futile attempt at choreography, 'We were sitting watching it all in a holding venue (it was closed roofed I remember) and watching it unfold on the big screen. Then suddenly the moment comes where all the nations are being invited to parade around. So then you start queuing up and it's all carefully orchestrated. We had a boy, girl, boy, girl line up of similar heights within each line. Not that you would know that watching us march in.

'I remember all the sailors were behind us so we were chatting to them and getting to know them and having a laugh. In front of me was Tim Henman. I kept walking into him every time [the parade slowed down] and eventually it got to the point where I was like, "I'm really sorry, could we have our picture taken with you?" And then we walked in and oh my God it was immense, far bigger than I ever imagined it would be.'

As each team completes their lap the athletes are corralled in the centre. In theory they're meant to stick neatly in their own teams. The reality is quite different, as the Sydney Olympian attests.

'You all go into a kind of holding area in the middle and then everything else kind of happens [around you]. There was such an atmosphere. You just wander around and meet different people. We went and found the Irish team, all five of them or however many there were, then we walked around with them and found all our mates in the Dutch team.'

Standing in the middle of the arena, sandwiched amongst 10,000 other athletes, the mind-boggling scale of the Olympic infrastructure hits home. Almost a quarter of the stadium's stands are devoted to studios and cameras for the world's media. Back home, TV networks have commenced two weeks of round the clock coverage. An army of volunteers help stage-manage proceedings on the track and scurry like ants across the stands.

Eventually the fireworks subside, the music quietens and the festival atmosphere in the huddle of athletes evaporates. It's time for the competition to begin.

The field of dreams or disappointment

For most athletes, the day following the opening ceremony is another jittery day's training down at the competition venue. The taper down from the big training volumes is complete. Now it's just a matter of staying sharp and not going crazy with the waiting. Before many pre-season competitions you're still too exhausted to get that nervous, but with the full Olympic taper everyone ends up bouncing off the walls, buzzing and feeling like caged tigers, endlessly pacing and waiting to be unleashed.

The first time you walk into your Olympic competition venue it's pretty special. As a post-Sydney friend of mine said, 'You walk in and know that this is it. I could come away with something amazing. This is what I've been aiming at for four years. I was always trying to look at all the colours and take in all the smells and everything.'

Yeah, drink it all in. Except the cheesy Olympic jingles played regularly over the loudspeakers. Thankfully the brain quickly tunes them out.

Experienced Olympians deal with this phase much better. Tom James competed in both Athens and Beijing, 'I felt a lot more relaxed for my second Olympics. I was quite overwhelmed when we arrived at the Athens venue. I was stressed. I wasn't dealing with it very well. Things were getting on top of me. I was putting all sorts of pressure on myself.'

With the help of their psychologists, athletes develop various coping mechanisms to try to deal with the intensity. Here's a medallist from Beijing. 'I quite consciously tried to make it feel like a World Championships venue because that was something I had lots of familiarity with, although inevitably with the whole security thing, the massive accreditation [checking] and scanning your bags each time, inevitably it brings home what a bigger-scale event the Olympics is. But as much as possible, you say to yourself this is just another day of training, this is just another set of races; we're just doing our job. I tried very consciously to not think about what the event was until the racing was finished.'

Others try and let off steam and amuse themselves to relieve the pressure. Here's Tom James again.

'Every day in Beijing we'd go in and out of security at the venue four times a day, doing our two training sessions. Each time I'd swap my accreditation with Hodgey. He's got long bright blonde [Viking like] hair and I've got dark short hair. They'd look at it and they'd just let you through – they genuinely couldn't tell the difference between English people!'

Rubbing shoulders with you at the venue are your competitors, the men and women looking to destroy you. Back home and on camp you've daily wondered how their campaigns are progressing. Are they pushing boundaries in training? Do they want it as much as you? Are their old injuries playing up? Most of them you know well, having sparred for years at previous World Championships, but the Olympics throws up the occasional new contender. For Beijing, the Chinese pulled together a whole variety of new teams outside their traditional sports. Likewise, South Korea put together a hockey team for Seoul in 1988. British hockey team member Steve Batchelor remembers the unsettling challenges of playing them, 'We hadn't set eyes on them before. That was a new experience for us. They were pretty rubbish but we still didn't do well against them.'

The modus operandi for operating at the Olympic venue precompetition is to appear to studiously avoid watching your competitors training and instead give off an air of complete unconcern and disinterest. Of course, behind dark sunglasses form and technique are carefully analysed from subtle glances. Inevitably, at some point you bump into your competitors at inescapably close quarters, coming out of the loo or in the showers. A polite nod and a quiet 'Hi' of recognition is all that is required. Blank them entirely and the childish return to schoolboy-style competition just gives the opposition more ammunition to feed their motivation. Worse, they might just laugh at you. Overfriendliness on the other hand can be read as weakness or a lack of respect for the event. And if you accidentally end up at adjacent urinals? Look silently ahead. No laughing, joking or staring. You'll be able to prove your dominance soon enough.

The pressure cooker

Athens
Mid August 2004

After all the waiting, all the training camps and the sacrifice, and the recent distractions of visits by Prime Ministers and drugs busts, I'm sitting in a quiet area of the warm-up tent and my Olympic final is just a few hours away. I've been training 11 years for this – even if I didn't know it for the first eight or so. I've done important races before but not like this. Not so life defining.

If I succeed, my many years in the sport will be crowned with an ultimate success. The narrative will work. But if I fail, then somehow everything that came before – all the previous cumulative successes needed to get here – they won't matter, because I couldn't cut it when it counted most.

I have this horrible feeling in my gut. A deep primal fear is swallowing me up – a desire to run, to be anywhere but here. For a minute I find myself envying Chimp. Having missed out he can sit at home and watch the racing. He isn't being judged today. No burning physical pain for him. Next my envy turns to another British teammate who has a deep and unwavering Christian faith and believes that whatever happens it is God's will. Whatever will be, will be. Must be immensely comforting to have the outcome in a higher power's hands.

To my left, Jamie reads his history book avidly. He prefers to distract himself until a few brief minutes before we start our physical warm-up. To my right, another teammate is plugged into his music and stares unseeing ahead of him. In his mind's eye he is rehearsing the race. He doesn't blink.

We are taking on the best in the world. They've trained for thousands of hours in their secretive foreign systems. Some are physiological freaks, far off the chart from normal. Others are legends in the sport, world record holders, previous Olympic champions or up and coming World Junior Champions. But what is most disconcerting, having seen them all practising, is that none of the competition looks scared in the least. They radiate confidence, focus and professionalism. I can smell no trace of fear on them. I hope I hid mine this past week.

My family and some close friends will be screaming from the stands, waving their specially purchased flags. My phone and Facebook page are clogged with messages, some from friends and some from people I lost touch with years ago. It seems as though everyone I've ever known is either in the crowd or watching on TV back home. Before the race they'll point me out to their friends.

But what about after my race? Will they shake their heads and say, 'Yeah, he always used to bottle it when it mattered'. Or will they be nodding and saying, 'Wow, he really stepped up. He was always amazing at school. No wonder I couldn't get near him!'

If I blunder in some horribly obvious way, disqualification after two false starts or another obvious fuck-up, people will forever be whispering behind my back at parties.

'Wasn't he at the Olympics?'

'Yes, he's the guy who …'

'Oh, that guy.' And they'll feel sorry for me. And not mention it.

And untold millions of people whom I've never met will form their view of me entirely from a few minutes of TV coverage. It's much harder to care or worry about them. I find myself drifting back to those characters who caused me pain in my past with whom I long ago lost contact. Will the ex-girlfriend whom I fell badly for when I was 17 be watching? Will she regret dumping me from a phone box on her way to meet her new man? And the maths teacher who humiliated me in front of the class when I was 13? Soon enough I can show them. I can put it all right.

Or were they right all along?

It's time to go through my mental preparation again; to lock my demons in their box with my rehearsed rational responses. I am the best I can be. I am the best I can be. I am the best I can be. You can't control the others. Who cares what anyone thinks of your performance but you? Are they in an Olympic final? Who are they to judge you?

All you have to do is spend yourself completely – and you can control that. Yes, it will hurt. It will be agony. But it's just a few minutes of agonising pain. Spend yourself utterly. Then what more can you have done? Ignore your body, when it says no more. When your muscles are screaming at you and your lungs are begging for air. Ignore them. Don't be afraid. You will not collapse. You will not die. YOU WILL NOT DIE. The training will get you through.

A series of deep breaths and I empty my mind. I feel calmer now, having briefly un-caged my fears and allowed them a canter before locking them back under. I can't wait for the physical pain. I'm almost praying for it to begin. It will be a welcome relief from this mental torture.

Ready for the biggest day of your life?

The day for which you've been preparing a decade or more is here; the pinnacle of your career, and probably your whole life. The terror coursing through your body a few hours before your Olympic final is literally breathtaking. Part of it is like the fear on the morning of your wedding day; the huge emotional journey, the need for everything to be perfect, your friends and family all watching and the terror of potential public embarrassment that comes with it. But this is much, much bigger than any wedding audience: 4.7 billion viewers watched the Beijing Olympics during its 17 days of competition – 4.7 BILLION. That's 70 per cent of the world's population: the largest TV audience ever known. Making the groom's speech after that should be child's play.

Add to the pre-wedding jitters the pressure you might feel before a career-defining pitch to the ultimate potential customer or the final round interview for the perfect job, one that you've long craved and know is ultra-competitive. This job interview only comes around every half decade and you might just get two shots at it in your life, three if you're very lucky. In team sports, the fear of letting teammates (who are often your closest friends) down is a major source of pressure. Fear of failure itself is terrifying for some. Seb Coe himself said it was the fear of failure that drove him. Literally running scared. Then stir in financial anxiety. The recognition that Olympic medals result in thousands of pounds or dollars of win bonuses, open up the lucrative corporate speaking circuit and the potential for product endorsements and advertising opportunities. Even the Olympic greats' Valhalla – a coveted spot in the TV commentary box.

Will you succeed? Or will you fail?

For most of the Western athletes the financial pressure is the least of it. After Beijing the gold medallists of Britain, Australia, Germany, Japan, Canada and the US could expect win bonuses from team sponsors or the government ranging between £10k to £25k. A nice sum but not a life changing one. For athletes from the developing and second world nations, however, a medal can lift them and their families out of poverty forever. Now that's pressure – racing for the livelihoods of your family and close friends.

The Russians have embraced capitalism and performance incentives – when visiting his Russian team in Beijing, Prime Minister Vladimir Putin announced that he was doubling the incentive programme – €100k for a gold, even €40k for a bronze. Some previous members of the Eastern Bloc are doing the same – Slovenians get around €40k for a gold medal, enough to buy a little house in the country. In Harare, Zimbabwean President Robert Mugabe presented his country's only Beijing gold medallist, the white swimmer Kirsty Coventry (who set a new world record in the 200m backstroke and also picked up three silver medals), with a suitcase filled with $100,000. Lucky for her they were US dollars; with Zimbabwe's hyperinflation they'd have been worth far less by the time she'd left the stage. Needless to say, she's not based in Zimbabwe but in the USA. I wonder if Mugabe saw the irony of his actions. Elsewhere, both Malaysian and South Korean medallists enjoy a medal bonus and then a lifetime pension. Palestinian Olympians also receive a pension-like allowance, even if it's only $100 a month.

But it's other Asian countries that provide the biggest incentives. In a bid to try to spur the country's athletes to a first gold medal the

Philippines put together an incredible win bonus of around 9.5 million pesos (c. $220k); 5 million was promised by the government (under the Incentives Act, which is written into Philippine law), with the remainder from wealthy Filipino individuals, such as boxer Manny Pacquiao and the founder of clothing company No Fear, alongside corporates such as Microsoft Philippines. It didn't work. The Philippines won no medals in Beijing. With Mongolia picking up a gold, the Philippines now holds the crown as the country with the most Olympic medals without a single gold.

A Thai gold medallist's package is worth more, around $314k, but the tiny nation of Singapore trumps this with a gold incentive bonus of £420,000 – although Singapore remains without a gold medal. But it is China that holds the crown, with a package reportedly worth over £1m. This includes 1kg of solid gold, £50k from a Hong Kong-based philanthropist, various bonuses from provincial governments and the General Administration of Sport, and a lifetime pension.

Regardless of their nation's financial incentives, every athlete feels immense pressure before their Olympic performance. How do they deal with it? Some don't. They break. They end up with their fingers in their ears rocking gently on the start line. Or they end up getting ill, stressing themselves to sickness. One Beijing silver medallist told me, 'You see it everywhere. In our athletes and other teams. You see erratic behaviour. Irrationality. High tension, short fuses. For some people, extreme quiet – going into your shell in an extreme way. The outcome? Poor performance.'

I asked Olympic gold medallist Tom James whether he'd seen people crack under pressure. Tom was in the British rowing eight in Athens, which came seventh, but won the gold four years later in Beijing in the four.

'Yeah, but when you say "cracked" it makes it sound as though it's like something sharp. But I think it manifests itself in gradual things which you probably don't notice. I didn't deal with Athens well at all. It's something I've learnt from. One of my teammates really fell apart. He'd have big mood swings. He'd shout at people. He'd make out he deserved better.'

In Athens he remembered the previous coxless four Olympic champions not having an easy ride. 'I remember seeing the four of them around the hotel, seeing Cracknell and Pinsent coming out of their rooms and it was obvious they've been crying. I spoke to Ed Coode (their crewmate) after they won. He said, "I really thought we were going to lose, those two were just falling apart."' That makes Matt Pinsent's floods of tears on the podium afterwards and his retirement easier to understand. If titans like Matt Pinsent and James Cracknell are crying with the pressure, what chances do mortals have? Another rower, on the women's team, found it strangely comforting. 'For our final we had to get up at about half five. I remember passing Matthew Pinsent sitting by the door waiting for his bus. He was there sipping on some Lucozade and he looked just dreadful. I looked at him and I thought, Okay this must be normal, this must be how you're meant to feel. It was reassuring to see such a great Olympian visibly suffering as much as I felt I was.'

Another Athens Olympian suffered similarly. 'I've never felt so nervous as before the final in Athens. I remember waking up in the night and going to the toilet and I thought I was really sick. I had to feel my way down the wall because I thought I was just going to collapse. I got back in to bed and I was thinking, some virus has just smacked me in the head, I am not going to be able to race. I felt fine when I went to bed and suddenly now I feel horrendous. Of course, I wasn't actually ill, it's just the response to the nerves and the body preparing to take on what you're about to do to it.'

Even if you get through the long, dark, lonely night before the final, the start line can be even more daunting. British triathlete Sian Brice was one of the three British women competing in the first-ever Olympic triathlon in Sydney 2000. It was a huge event.

'The girls' triathlon was the first race to go off on the first day of the Sydney Games. It was a blockbuster launch, against the backdrop of Sydney harbour and the Opera House. Australia was the biggest place for triathlon in the world at the time. The Aussies were expecting a medal.' It wasn't an unreasonable expectation, Brice had come sixth in the previous year's World Championships behind five Australians, only three of whom could enter the Olympics. So Brice, too, was a real medal shot.

On the start pontoon she remembers, 'I was over-nervous, scared nervous which was not good. I don't know how I'd got myself into that position. The coaches were slightly overawed by the Olympics as well. We were quite a disparate team – I remember sitting alone eating dinner the night before the race. And I'd also got my knickers in a twist about the draw for the pontoon start.'

Each of the 50 triathletes has their own half metre start area on a pontoon. As Sian says, 'The positioning is quite crucial – if you're next to a good swimmer, that's great,' as they can help pull you along the swim.

'Everybody knows who the good swimmers are so it's quite tactical. The top 12 in the world traditionally have a kind of advantage – picking their start positions and being able to see where those ahead in the draw have picked. But they made us [the top 12] draw blind so we couldn't see what positions others had picked – whereas the next 24 could see where we all were and then see each of them placed electronically on the pontoon. So it was a disadvantage to be in the top 12 in the world. Number 18, or whoever, could see where the two best swimmers were and could pick the spot next to them. Maybe I used my brain too much. But I was cross – how did they decide this? This is not right! Can't you see it's not right?'

The Olympics is just as good at serving up distractions as it is nerves. And the stresses of the situation can manifest themselves physically, just when you want to be at your peak. Nick Bell, twice a member of the

British fencing team, was well qualified to assess the physical effects of stress as a medical doctor.

'I couldn't eat properly before an event. We used to routinely get diarrhoea. And several of us used to get lots of cold sores, usually after the event, with the release of stress from the body.'

Others get colds and sore throats, with the stress straining the immune system under pressure. Most athletes sleep terribly, but the Australian Olympic gold medallist I spoke to slept worst than most before her Atlanta Olympic final.

'A bomb went off the night before we raced in Central Park. The same night we also had a bomb threat at the military base we were staying at. It came through at 2am and they evacuated us. We never got back into our room. We spent the night sitting on the pavement outside. I hadn't got any sleep at all. Not a minute. I remember thinking – why tonight? Why the day of my Olympic final? But I realised I couldn't be negative – so I tapped my teammate on the shoulder – "time to carbo load" and we sat there eating bananas. Lucky for us we packed our bags the night before.'

The day of competition itself brings no respite. One silver medallist recalled, 'It's that pit in your stomach. You wake up with it and you feel it grow through the day. The worst is waiting at the venue before you start your warm-up. You're just sitting there ready to go but you can't do anything. You see other competitors head off for their races. And a little later you can hear the crowd roar them home, with some becoming Olympic champions. That's tough. It gives you that sick feeling.'

Everyone responds to the pressure differently. Hockey player Steve Batchelor didn't get stressed until his Olympics was finished.

'Before a game I didn't feel too nervous. I liked messing around. I was always known as the joker. The only time I completely lost it, when I got really nervous, was the final. Not before it, but when I got taken off with 20 minutes to go. We were 3–1 up. I knew we pretty much had it in the bag but I hid behind the dugout and couldn't watch it at all.'

Steve was very unusual. Most feel the terror before the performance, not after. Given the inevitable distractions and the real physical impact pressure can have on Olympians it's no wonder they turn to experts to help them with their mental preparation. Experts in the art of mind control.

Yoda and the head doctors

The Olympics began in ancient Greece, around 776 BC. Contestants, coaches, masseurs and supporters travelled to Olympia from all over the Greek world to compete in the festival and honour Zeus, the King of the Gods. And so it continued, once every four years or so, until about the third century AD. By then Greece's power had waned, whilst Rome's had risen. The Roman Emperor Theodosius, a Christian, banned the sporting tribute to the old gods around 394 AD.

Coaches and physiotherapists (or at least masseurs) were just as common when the modern Olympics were re-ignited by Baron Pierre de Coubertin in 1896. Sports psychology and sports psychologists on the other hand are a relatively new Olympic phenomenon. Today, along with physiologists, nutritionists, physiotherapists, coaches, performance directors and team managers, they are ubiquitous across the major Olympic teams. But outside of elite sport no one knows what they do. There's an aura of brainwashing and black magic about the practice, but it's more like learning the ways of the Jedi.

The discipline began in the USA in the 1920s but only really started to take off in the latter half of the century. The East Germans were experimenting with the ideas and concepts in the 1960s and '70s, leaving no stone unturned in their search for sporting victory to support the political agenda. By the 1980s, sports psychology had started emerging from the shadows in the United States. Then the Australian Institute of Sport latched onto it in the 1990s, followed by Great Britain later that decade.

I sought out Dr Chris Shambrook, one of Team GB's leading sports psychologists to lift the veil on what they do. Over 15 years he's worked with elite golfers, county cricketers, premiership footballers and at three Olympics (Sydney, Athens and Beijing) with Team GB working across a variety of sports. He is helping prepare some of the athletes for 2012. Chris is in his 40s with a thin, focused face and looks as fit as one of his athletic charges. I met him between corporate engagements. In between Games, and thanks in part to the success of his Olympic charges, he's taken the mental training methodologies from elite sport into the corporate world, with his performance consultancy firm K2. With their corporate clients they, 'apply performance principles that are utilised and taken for granted in the world of elite sport to optimise performance. Getting people to see themselves as performers rather than fulfilling a role at work.' You might think they would be focused on big salespeople, looking to boost their confidence before an important sales pitch but I was surprised to find they've worked with everyone from CEOs right across to the call centre teams of a large insurance company.

The first thing to understand is that there are both psychologists and psychiatrists working in sport, although much fewer of the latter. Psychiatrists are clinically trained and treat mental disorders or imbalances. The British cycling team works with a psychiatrist called Dr Steve Peters, who has previously treated severe personality disorders at Rampton High Security Hospital, which houses the likes of Charles Bronson and Ian Huntley. As Shambrook says, 'They [psychiatrists] come from the perspective of fixing broken people. There are some pretty intense pressures which elite athletes are going to face. If there are chinks in your armour it's a good idea to have faced them, to have looked at the demons or neuroses you might have which you need to get control of.'

But sports psychologists are different and much more prevalent at the top level of sport. Rather than confronting neuroses, their approach is more akin to the day-to-day Olympic training – but working on 'mental fitness' and thinking skills.

Understandably, a robust psychology is vital in Chris's view: 'Taking the Olympic 100m final, they're all similarly trained physically. There is some physiological variation but it's within a small population – the distribution within the elite. They are all able to run similar times. So it's down to who holds their nerve best on the day – it's who knows their mental recipe best to let it all be delivered absolutely when it matters most.'

One aspect of the psychologist's art is to prevent athletes choking.

'Choking is a good example of how the situation you find yourself in starts controlling your thought processes,' says Chris Shambrook. 'Because you've got yourself in a winning position all of a sudden you're much more thoughtful. You start second guessing. You start trying to think your way through rather than naturally trusting the same approach that got you into that winning position. You start thinking and using your brain in a way you hadn't until that point. You become very outcome-focused rather than process-focused. You are no longer completely immersed in the moment.'

Pete Sampras was a master of not choking; you don't win 14 Grand Slams otherwise. And a master of being in the moment – having won one of his many important matches he was asked what was going through his mind at the match's fulcrum, on a key second serve which he aced. He thought for a moment and confirmed, 'There was absolutely nothing going through my mind at the time.'

That's being in the moment.

With victory in sight that's when sportspeople really show their mental discipline and it can be this trait alone that separates gold medallists from the rest. 'After all,' says Shambrook, 'it's very obvious what outcome you're absolutely passionate about getting – but you have to ignore it, right up the point that you actually may have got it.'

It's a very tough thing to do: 3–1 up in the last five minutes of the Olympic hockey final or 10ft up on the field in the home straight of the 800m, you'd be inhuman not to think about victory. But you've got to be inhuman. A ruthless, high-performing robot. A robot that is totally in the moment. One that doesn't think – certainly never about winning. This is quite an alien concept. Thoughts and emotions are just what happen in your head in response to the world around you, right? Sports psychology takes a different view; you can train yourself to think and react differently and change your emotions. More Jedi mind tricks. Chris says you can practise to 'choose your body language and choose positive self talk'. That internal monologue going on in your head – you can train him or her. And you can train yourself to control your emotions to improve performance. As Yoda would say, 'Anger, fear, aggression: the dark side of the force are they.'

Chris continues, 'You've got to practise that ability to immerse yourself completely and be able to trust that it gives you the best chance of delivering. You spend all that time being coached, coached, coached in training. Now you're racing. Go. Forget and trust.'

Or as Obi-Wan Kenobi teaches Luke Skywalker in Star Wars, 'Let go of your conscious self and act on instinct.'

You sometimes hear amateur tennis players or Sunday league footballers finish their games and, after a good session, say, 'I was really in the zone'. And sporting professionals refer to the magical state too – Mike Atherton, a long-serving England cricket captain, describes the final afternoon of his greatest innings in his autobiography *Opening Up*. 'For the only time in my career I was in the zone … while I can describe my feeling, I couldn't begin to explain how to replicate it … I was in an almost trance-like state. It was a state of both inertia and intense concentration and I knew that I was in total control and they couldn't get me out.' The result? An innings of 185 not out and a drawn Test with South Africa in 1995.

I ask Shambrook – is there really a zone?

'In the literature it's called a flow state. There are those times when the performer hits an optimum state and everything works. Time tends to feel like it's passing more slowly. You feel like you can predict what is going to happen. You feel completely in control but you are totally immersed in what you are doing. And you will not have much memory of it afterwards.'

Atherton's quote also touches on the importance of confidence, a vital part of elite performance, which sports psychologists work hard to develop in their charges. Shambrook elucidates.

'The whole confidence area is critical. It's taken for granted that because athletes can do all these things physically and technically they should be super-confident. But they don't necessarily take that step for themselves. You spend a huge amount of time working on stuff that isn't good enough and getting criticised, and this doesn't do a great deal for your belief in yourself.'

Having got to know quite a few elite athletes I can recognise what Chris says. Ridiculous as it may seem, many on the world stage really don't believe their sporting technique is actually very good. After all, coaches spend every waking moment correcting you. Some world bronze and silver medallists genuinely believed they simply didn't have it in them to win. I personally thought my technique was pretty average. Ridiculous as it may seem, confidence is a real problem in elite performers. Shambrook agreed.

'What you see from very good, mentally tough performers is not necessarily that they are super-confident. It's that the confidence they do have does not get undermined quickly or easily. Slight things going wrong do not make them start doubting themselves. Other performers, who are not as resilient in their confidence – when something doesn't go to plan, their confidence is more like a house of cards.'

It's easy to spot a team or an athlete who's lost their belief. Negativity and doubt take hold and are radiated by gloomy body language. Performance plummets. Pessimism spreads like a virus. Once it's taken hold of a team or squad it's very hard to cure. After all, how can you believe anything the coach says, when he got you into this mess?

Contrast that with the football teams of José Mourinho. Mourinho is the self-proclaimed Special One of European football. His teams benefit not just from his coaching, but from his immense, unshakable and, let's be frank, rather annoying self-belief. They run onto the pitch knowing there is a mastermind at work on their touchline. During the game they believe unquestioningly in every change of tactics José dictates, while back on the training ground, every technical suggestion is accepted and worked on without question.

As one American gold medallist told me, 'Everybody on the start line in the final has promised their mother they're going to win – but only one is. We knew we were going to win, everyone [in the final] knows they're going to win. I don't think you can win a race unless you know that.' It's partly a trained suspension of disbelief, partly pig-headedness but mostly massive self-confidence that is needed.

Confidence can provide real physiological benefits, as one silver medallist I spoke to confirmed, 'Before the final in Beijing there was certainly a lot of pressure. I was nervous, sure, but I slept really well the night before because I was confident. There were lots of races in my career when I didn't sleep well the night before but by the time Beijing rolled around I felt I knew what I had to do.'

And the reverse is true, physiological changes can alter your psychological state. It's natural to assume it is a one way street – your mood drives your body language – but your body language also affects your mood. For example, several studies have shown that partici-pants holding a pencil in their teeth, which activates the muscles used for smiling, actually become happier. And it's not just the silliness of having a pencil in your mouth – participants holding a pencil between their lips (which doesn't activate the smile muscles) get no such benefit to their mood.

So, even if it feels that failure is inevitable, walk tall, hold your head high, maintain normal levels of eye contact and you'll actually start feeling more confident. In turn, positive body language helps main-tain and build the confidence of teammates, and coaches whose upbeat vibes feed your own beliefs – a positive feedback loop. But it works the other way too. One or two disbelievers and soon a whole team can have its confidence cut out like an apple core.

When thinking about confidence and sport, preening prima donnas immediately spring to mind. I asked Shambrook, isn't there a thin line between resilient confidence and a big ego?

'You'll often find the top performers are the ones who have big egos but it's justified. The evidence is there – they are the best in the world. But you find the greatest are able to carry off that great level of confidence without it leading to complacency. Others may have some successes and get a bit ahead of themselves. They start getting distracted by the other stuff that comes with the success which stops them focusing on the recipe that got them there in the first place.' Several cocky starlets that fell from grace as quickly as they emerged spring to mind.

One of the Los Angeles Olympians I spoke to (who, to put it in context, wasn't a medallist) was pretty damning about the personalities of gold medallists. 'If you look at winners in any sport they're actually not very nice people. Ego doesn't make the nicest people in the world but it does make winners. I've had 40 years in sport and have athlete friends all round the world but the really top ones you don't particularly engage with, it's the next rung down who are more human, who you keep in touch with.'

For most of us, without natural, unshakable self-belief, psychologists help build robust confidence based on evidence. On my head doctor's advice I kept detailed training diaries, religiously filling them in after each session – weights lifted, split times achieved, technical focuses and progress. I monitored performance and progress across three dimensions – physiological, technical and mental. The diaries provided real evidence of tangible progress, which was hugely motivating, particularly on cold, dark and rainy winter days, months before the racing season. Before competition it was reassuring to review them and remind myself the extent of my preparation: a great way of building robust confidence.

But how can you try to build the confidence that you're going to win, when the evidence says you're going to lose? Maybe it's a quarter final of the Olympic tennis and you come up against a girl you've lost to three times previously? I put it to Chris Shambrook.

'It's not just confidence in winning. More important is your belief in your ability to execute the task. Most sports performers want confidence they can win – but you can't cut straight to that when there's no evidence you can. You need to have confidence in your ability to consistently execute the skills needed to give yourself the best chance. And to be able to do that in all performance conditions. And then you see where that gets you relative to the competition.'

In other words, you've got to believe, otherwise failure is inevitable.

More Yoda-like teachings, reminiscent of the scene in *The Empire Strikes Back* where Jedi Master Yoda challenges Luke Skywalker to a seemingly impossible task.

'OK, I'll give it a try,' replies Luke, deflated at the impossibility of the task.

Yoda stops him. 'No, try not. Do … or do not, there is not try.'

Luke tries, struggles and fails. The diminutive Yoda frowns and completes the task.

Luke, incredulous, 'I don't believe it'

Yoda completes the lesson, 'That is why you failed.'

Tom James won Olympic gold in the men's coxless four in Beijing, filled with the belief that, while they weren't perfect, they were good enough. His recall of the last few weeks before his final chimes with Shambrook's (and Yoda's) comments.

'I remember going out to Beijing thinking I've no idea how we're going to do. We'd had lots of injuries in training. Lower back problems, some of the guys having to have epidurals. It really wasn't until Beijing that we started clicking. Then we started building up confidence, Jurgen [his coach] is very good at that. That's why I trust him. He knows when he's looking at your crew whether it's good enough to win the

Olympics. That's very important. So many coaches make the mistake of wanting something absolutely perfect, something brilliant – so you're constantly looking for this thing which in reality is unachievable. You're constantly stressing about it being not quite good enough to win. That's what Jurgen does well. We'd go out and some things wouldn't be quite right but he'd tell us to relax, this is good, stop stressing. And actually having a coach confirming the boat is moving well, rather than constantly looking for something more is very reassuring. You can't go into a final not knowing how you're going to perform. You need to know that you can put in a good race, but you can't do that by fretting about the small things. It comes from being free and being confident and natural, rather than worrying about the outcome.'

And on the day of the big race Shambrook believes you should warm up your mind, just like you'd warm up your muscles. 'Mentally warming up for a performance is really important. Physical and technical warm-up takes place consistently but you also need to be able to get your head from whatever state you have woken up in to completely in the right place. You are not guaranteed to wake up on the morning of the Olympic final feeling brilliant.' Quite the opposite, in fact. You feel terrible – mentally, emotionally and physically.

But as Shambrook teaches his charges, 'You can choose to change your thought processes, change your moods and change your feelings so that you're completely ready and focused to go. You need to be the consistent factor in an inconsistent environment. Having a trusted routine to get you in control when you want to get in control, is essential. And you need to practise the routine religiously in training and at competitions.

'The routine is helpful in dealing with pressure. Self-awareness is a critical component here – understanding your personality and how you respond to pressure. The pressure comes from different places. It isn't the pressure of the Olympics that does things to people, it's the pressure of what the Olympics means to each person and it also depends on their personality. To deal with pressure you've got to understand the source. There are the obvious inbuilt factors like this is only every four years and if you mess it up you've got a long time to wait, but the personal variation is probably more important. Someone who might be very motivated by their nearest and dearest having a positive view of them would have a different response to someone who is driven to create a legacy of being the best in the world.'

Routine was important to my preparation before each race, making me feel in control and ready. A Beijing silver medallist I spoke to echoed this. 'I'm a person of routine. Most athletes are. Routine helps to reinforce the fact that your performance day is just the same as a training day. So for me it was about knowing and repeating that routine. The warm-up. The stretching routine. The music I'd listen to. All those things would be consistent over a long period of time.' And the music? 'For Beijing it was DJ Milo. That was that season's warm-up music.'

When I asked whether his warm-up was just full of superstitions, the silver medallist put me back in my place. 'No, no lucky socks. There was a phase in my career where I had loads of little superstitions. But the longer I stayed competing the more I felt it was counter-productive and the more it made sense to have routines which gave you a helpful rhythm without the silly superstitions.'

Alongside robust confidence, an ability to control thoughts and be absolutely in the moment, the other key skills sports psychologists teach are mental rehearsal of performance, concentration and critical thinking. Or as Shambrook puts it, 'You need to be skilful at evaluating and objectively reviewing what your next steps are – not being overly emotional or responsive to the result of a heat, for example'.

Shambrook highlights concentration skills above all else, 'To be great you need to absolutely focus on the right thing at the right time and to keep out inappropriate factors and distraction'. This skill really comes to the fore at the Olympics, with more potential distractions than any other sporting event.

Dutch volleyball player Bas van de Goor highlighted an extreme example of this ability to me. On the first day of Olympic competition in Beijing, the father-in-law of the US men's volleyball coach was stabbed and killed by a lone Chinese assailant without apparent motive. Says Bas, 'He was well known in the volleyball scene. Everybody knew him.' The team were distraught. Their coach flew home to be with his wife in the USA.

'Before the Olympics, their mental coach had worked with them on how to perform if the conditions were not 100 per cent. You can imagine that, at that point, conditions were 0 per cent. A week later their coach returned and the USA won the gold medal as an outsider. It's the best example I know of coping with extreme bad luck and the benefit of mental coaching to focus on things you can influence.'

Rounding off the main strands of sports psychology, there is the sport-specific mental preparation, as Chris Shambrook explained: 'For combat sports – am I mentally ready to get hurt and get hit? Boxing is terrifying for people who don't box, because you're not mentally prepared for that. For endurance sports, the ability to push through a pain barrier and the knowledge of how much you're going to hurt yourself and prepare for that is key. For team sports, there's a lot around relationships with teammates and the ability to trust and work with them, the ability to connect with others and play your part.'

But despite a gradually broadening recognition of the importance of the mind, there is still a lot of scepticism amongst Olympians about the head doctors and their teachings, and some athletes see their use as a weakness. It's a very individual choice. One guy in a team will buy into the doctrine, the next, perhaps with a very similar background and level of experience, won't.

Triathlete Sian Brice, for example, outlined her team's approach pre-Sydney. 'We actually didn't have much psychology support. I never really questioned that. You could if you were really losing the plot but I personally was not that dependent on a psychologist. I was quite strong-minded, and because I'd competed internationally as a child, I was used to pressure situations. Sure, sometimes I put too much pressure on myself and got it wrong, but I was capable of working it out for myself.'

Part of some athletes' scepticism is no doubt due to the psychologists' craft being both invisible and difficult to measure. The truth is many of the great athletes, and the great coaches, are masters of the dark arts of the mind without specialist help – either being self-taught or just innately having the core foundations. They are just supremely confident. Experiences in their formative years made them able to control their emotions to the point of being automatons, until they cross the line at least. They do sports psychology, without calling it sports psychology.

Many of the less supreme athletes ape the attitude of the greats, probably to their cost. As a mere mortal, I found much of the head doctors' teachings useful. The confidence tricks, the tracking of performance with training diaries, the routines, the management and understanding of pressure. Without the Yodas of Team GB, the Olympics and the unique set of pressures it brings would have been overwhelming.

the performance

Is that it?

Athens
Mid August 2004

A minute after crossing the line my muscles have lessened their screaming and my desperate lungs have pulled in enough air to lift me from unthinking primal agony. That was it. My Olympics.

I can hear the winners exploding with emotion but I'm strangely numb. Is that really it? It was over so quick. My brain automatically switches to dissecting the race, technically and tactically, to adjust for the next competition. The realisation that there isn't a 'next competition' does not compute. There's a short circuit in the wiring.

It wasn't perfect, a long way from it. It wasn't even particularly good. Half way through, despite all the mental preparation with the psychologist, I knew I was out of the running and that recognition made it doubly impossible to recover. For a split second, two thirds through, I was aware of my coach on the sidelines. I swear I heard his voice. A sober and charitable cheer of encouragement but the hopelessness and disappointment pierced the cacophony and intensity of the moment. It added to the weight of the pointlessness of my position.

My head is in my hands. The same expletive comes out quietly and robotically. I can't believe it. There is still a fiery residue when I inhale but the intensity of the muscle pain has ebbed gradually away to a fierce ache, more than replaced by mental anguish which becomes heavier and heavier. I wish I had just crossed the line again, into the blissful acid bath of agony which makes thought impossible.

After a dark eternity I decide I have to brave reality and pull my hands from my face. Looking up and to one side, I see one of the crowd, a tearful mother wrapped in a flag, being helped across the barriers. She dodges past two uncertain volunteers to embrace her Olympian son in an almighty wraparound hug. Heads on each others' shoulders, they sob with joy, lost in emotion and totally unaware of the thousands watching their private moment. Somewhere up there is my family. They came a long way to watch nothing of note from their sibling and son.

Would a perfect race have been enough? I don't think so. They were just so damn fast. Even if I didn't believe it I'd have to try to convince myself of that or I'd go mad with self-disgust.

What do I do now? I resist the normal post-race reflex to do a warm down. No point, no training session tomorrow.

I want to do something, anything. I know that I should have and I could have done better. But there is nothing to be done. That was it. C'est fini. Games over.

I suppose I should go and have a shower?

Poles apart

Eleven thousand into 300 just does not go. Only a fraction of the thousands of Olympians come away with gold. At a modern summer Games, there are almost 1,000 medal slots, around 300 gold, the same number of silver and 350 or so bronzes, as combat sports like boxing award them to the two losing semi-finalists.

It's not about the medals though, not really. Like me, many Olympians go into competition knowing they have no realistic chance of a medal. Hey, it's always nice to hope but medals are garnish. I've known genuinely happy quarter finalists who've just been knocked out, and publicly politely excited gold medallists who are privately seething at themselves for perceived underperformance. When it comes down to it, the only criteria that really matters and which only the athlete can judge, is:

Did I give it everything? Did I fulfil my potential?

This puts Olympians in two camps after competition.

1. I had a great Olympics. I did everything I could or, as a French non-medallist neatly summed up: 'We did our best. No regrets.' This is the camp you really want to be in. They sleep a lot better.

The alternative:

2. I messed up. I'm an idiot. I wasted my shot.

I haven't met an Olympian yet who has said, 'Yeah, it went OK.'

Triathlete Sian Brice is a subscriber to this logic.

'If you can wake up the next morning, look yourself in the mirror and know you did your best, well, that is all you can do. It sounds clichéd but when I was really nervous that understanding was the best way of controlling it. I had my best ever race at the World Championships in Montreal almost exactly a year to the day before the Olympics. I wanted to cross that line with every part of my body in pain and that's what I wanted to achieve and that's what I did. That last two minutes of running, every single time I lifted my leg it was a massive effort. I could just about see fifth ahead and I knew the next competitor was only 10m behind me. When I crossed the line every single part of me hurt. Everything. I leant against this fence and it was just agony. Someone said, "You almost caught up fifth!" but I wasn't bothered, even though I'd have got something like another ten grand of lottery funding. If you're top five in the world you get a big increase. I was sixth but I didn't care because I knew I couldn't have gone one inch harder. Ultimately I had pushed myself to my limit and that was massively satisfying more than anything else. I know that was my best race ever.'

Poor Sian didn't get to enjoy the same satisfaction at the Olympics, crashing out on the bike, breaking her ribs and not being allowed to continue. Understandably, she was devastated but even medallists can look miserable on the podium, standing up there at the peak of their athletic careers. At the summit of mine, on the podium at a World Championship, I look like I'm chewing a wasp. Take note medallists: smile even if you don't achieve what you hoped. None of the viewing public warm to a grumpy medallist and in years to come you'll regret the face you pulled every time you pass the mantelpiece. Even if you're distraught inside put a brave face on, like this bronze medallist and her team in Beijing who missed gold by a margin of less than 0.1 per cent:

'Going onto the podium we agreed to make sure that to the outside world we looked like we'd done something which we were pretty proud of. Obviously we and our close friends and family knew how we actually felt about it. I always remember seeing some British athletes in Atlanta when they came third and they just looked so miserable on the podium. As an outsider you think, "Why are you so miserable, you've just won a medal?"'

Having talked to many Olympians about their experiences, some good, some disastrous, there seems to be a memory bias. Those who, in their view, succeeded recount a more detailed memory of the Olympic experience. Those who feel they failed recall much less. Listen to this athlete who came last in his field in Athens.

'It's not good for you to ask me questions about the lead up to Athens because I've repressed most of the experience. Honestly. I just don't remember it. In my particular situation in the lead up to Athens I felt the psychology was sufficiently wrong between me, the team and the coaching staff that I wasn't engaged in the experience in a way that I remember. I remember bits but none of the lead up.'

Makes for a difficult interview.

The Olympics is a rollercoaster of emotion for gold medallists too. Granted much more enjoyable emotions, but equally exhausting in their own way. I asked an American gold medallist what he felt when he crossed the line first at a home Games in Los Angeles.

'Relief, honestly. Sheer utter relief. I'd been at it pretty hard for 13 years. I really loved my sport for the first 11. The last two were just grinding it out. You can't quit because you know the finish line is close but you really want to. It wasn't that much fun. Then when you win, you know you never have to do it again if you don't want to. You know your time has been well spent. Your family is so happy and that's a wonderful thing, but honestly just sheer utter relief. Thank God that's over. Finally you can close that chapter on your life.'

An Aussie gold medallist from Atlanta struggled to make sense of her emotion after the closing seconds of her final.

'The Americans were closing, closing, closing. The last 250m I was willing on every part of my body. There was just nothing more to give. Then the line came. I didn't know who won. It was the one time I downloaded myself 100 per cent, unfortunately I wouldn't say I did that in my other two Olympics. Then it came up on the board. A heartbeat ahead of them. I mean, you dream for things to happen. It felt, it felt, it felt … simply awesome. I had someone pinch me to check it wasn't a dream because it's just so beyond comprehension that it happened. Singing the national anthem wasn't quite so awesome. I was really conscious of how bad I was singing. You've got no voice from competing [and crying] and I got kicked out of choir at school.'

Beijing champion Tom James brings another perspective to crossing the line first.

'To be honest it was quite un-dramatic after we crossed the line. I don't remember getting that feeling of elation which usually comes from winning a race. I think because we had gone in to the final as favourites there was a feeling of "We should win this provided we don't screw it up" – so when we then won it was a feeling of relief and job done as opposed to "Holy shit, I'm now an Olympic gold medallist". It's almost too big a thing to take in during that one moment. Seeing everyone's reactions on the bank came as quite a surprise. For the spectators the race had obviously been very exciting and it looked like we weren't going to win for most of the race. In the boat though it was quite calm and clinical and quite unemotional.

'You put the achievement of winning a gold medal, including the people who win them, on such a high pedestal that when you yourself win, it automatically diminishes your perception of the achievement. Just after finishing I remember thinking, what was all the fuss about? It was just another race with normal people rowing in boats. I previously put the Olympics into a special category in my head which says everything about it is perfect, everyone rows brilliantly, everyone is awesome and will have the race of their lives. In reality that's not the case – it's just a race, just like all the other races I've done in my life.

'And yet, the hours after the race were quite surreal. I was pretty exhausted, very mentally fatigued and simply wasn't able to absorb everything going on. I remember interview after interview and suddenly it was 3am and I was on a BBC show with Gabby Logan. It wasn't till I got home and back to a normal lifestyle a couple of weeks after, back to my house in Wales and sitting round with my parents, that things sort of sunk in.'

You bump into gold medallists like Tom in the Village wandering in a zombie-like daze, having won their medal that morning, or in the showers at the competition venue, where I saw a medallist ask another competitor, 'Do I take the medal off or do I leave it on?' So gobsmacked was he at having it he didn't know whether he should shower with it on or off.

Nature or nurture?

Watching your machine-like competitors break down with emotion on the Olympic podium you end up asking yourself some uncomfortable questions. Did I ever actually have what it takes? What does it take to make the podium? I asked other Olympians the same question.

In his wonderful book *Outliers*, Malcolm Gladwell looks at men and women who sit far outside the normal distribution of humanity and asks, why? Why were The Beatles the biggest rock band in history? What made Bill Gates one of the last century's most successful software entrepreneurs and one of the world's richest men? Why isn't Chris Langan, an American who has an IQ of 195, a billionaire? To put Langan's IQ in perspective, an average IQ is between 90 and 110; 140 or above is defined as genius. Why then is Langan a bouncer?

One of Gladwell's central arguments is that practice makes perfect. Practice makes outliers. Specifically, to be really great at something, whether it's composing concertos or writing software, you need to have practised a lot – he called it the 10,000 hour rule. It was the amount of practice that the outliers had done in relation to their peers that made them great. And it was the background of these outliers – their culture, their family history and their timing (no point being born Bill Gates in the 18th century) that allowed them to complete the magical 10,000 hours of practice.

Table tennis international turned *Times* writer, Matthew Syed, echoed the sentiment in his book *Bounce*. The sub-title of the book – 'The myth of talent and the power of practice' – puts across his stance neatly. Syed's argument in *Bounce* is certainly seductive. We can all be great if we practise. Harvard Professor Steven Jay Gould seems to agree, and has said, 'Any achievement at any sport is all about hard work.'

In part, I wrote this book to give me an excuse to seek out and interview great people, outliers in their own way and to find out how and why they got there. I'm not alone. We are all hypnotised by greatness. Bookshops are full of biographies promising insight into the secrets of greatness and self-help manuals outlining the magical habits that result in success, wealth and happiness. *Mediocrity – a study in average* has yet to hit the top of the bestseller list.

So I asked Olympians to consider the small percentage of Olympic athletes who made the podium, the highest performers and greatest outliers, and asked what was different about them. Was it talent (i.e.

genetic) or practice? Or, at the top level, is it all in the mind? Or even, whisper it, given the tiny margins that split the medallists from the also rans, isn't it just luck?

It's all in the genes

The breadth of natural genetic variation in sport hit me aged 17. The British selectors had sent in a physiologist to measure our top guys. We'd trained with heart rate monitors before and I knew how our heart rates varied. Most of the guys could hit more than 200 beats per minute when flat out. Mine was slower and I presumed bigger but it seemed to get the job done. We knew which of us could lift bigger weights and who was quickest over different distances. But for the first time that day we had blood samples taken between work-outs. This was our first real insight into ourselves, into our own chemical engines. The efficiency of our lungs, heart and circulation systems and how they compared to others.

When I read down the list of results on the notice board a few days later I was surprised. Our hematocrit scores, whatever that was, varied wildly. Mine was only average. It was lower than the fastest guy by a good margin. Nick had a hematocrit level of just over 50 per cent (53 per cent if I remember correctly). Mine was in the low 40s. In later tests the relative difference was similar.

That afternoon I had two questions for my coach.

'What is hematocrit?'

'The concentration of red blood cells in your blood.'

Second question.

'How do I improve it? How do I get a level like Nick?'

The response was simple, 'You can't really. It's basically genetic.'

That didn't seem very fair to me. Each pint of blood his heart pumped around carried 13 per cent more oxygen-carrying red blood cells. His hematocrit level would have got him banned from the Tour de France.

Was he on EPO? Back then we didn't even know what EPO was. Had he done thousands of hours more training than me and somehow increased his EPO levels? No, since the age of 13 we'd done exactly the same training schedule, give or take a few days lost to illness here or there. Nick had a reputation for being tougher than anyone else amongst us. But was it his system that allowed him to keep going, as we all fell behind?

Around 25,000 genes form the blueprint of each of us. No one is sure yet precisely how many – genetics is still a young science and enormously complex. As each gene interacts with other genes, the number of potential combinations and their outcomes are practically infinite.

Genetics determines physical characteristics like our sex, eye and hair colour, and the DNA blueprint also heavily influences our personality and mental health. If properly fed and reasonably healthy in childhood, our height is largely genetically determined (by the interplay of at least one hundred different genes). Height is important in almost every sport. Being tall in basketball is obviously helpful – the taller player can more easily block the shorter player, taller players' shots have less distance to travel to hit the basket and they can pick up rebounds more easily. Likewise volleyball, where taller players can spike the ball down into an opponent's half at a sharper angle. In baseball, taller pitchers are throwing from a higher angle (throwing slightly downhill); they release the ball closer to the batter and use their longer legs to power their pitch speed. Many successful fast bowlers in cricket are of above average height – the higher release point allowing for better bounce. In tennis, whilst there have been great players both tall and short, the top four men in the world today are all above 6ft, height helping service angle and power, and longer arms allowing them to get to more shots. In weight-lifting, in contrast, being short is advantageous. Within each weight class, the shorter athletes have less distance to lift the bar with their shorter levers (arms, legs and back).

Genetics provides other mechanical advantages. Swimmer Michael Phelps has size 14 feet, which act like flippers, hands like soup plates that allow him to develop more force against the water, and he is 'ape positive' – his arm span is three inches greater than his height. Longer arms allow for more leverage through the water and a relatively shorter torso produces less drag. Leonardo da Vinci's Vitruvian Man is ape neutral, with an arm span exactly equal to his height.

Genetics conveys not only obvious mechanical advantages but also invisible secret weapons which science has only just started to explore in the last few decades; lung capacity, for example. One of the Olympians I met had, at one time, the biggest pair of lungs ever measured. Perhaps these were even more crucial to Josh West's rowing success, beyond his height and albatross-like arm span, the latter providing extra leverage for the rowing stroke. Lung capacity doesn't really change with training. What genetics gives you, you're stuck with. And bigger lungs allow greater oxygen intake, allowing greater aerobic performance.

'I always felt I was genetically superior,' Josh says with a wink. 'Each athlete has their own way round these things in their head. Another person in the team had the view genetics didn't matter at all. I had the view that actually I was better than most genetically.'

Who can argue?

Another rower, Sir Matt Pinsent, the four-time Olympic gold medallist, held the crown for the biggest British lungs until Josh arrived. Pinsent's lungs had a volume of 8.5 litres, about 50 per cent bigger the average (i.e. an extra lung compared to most adult males). For comparison, two of the most successful Tour de France cyclists, Lance Armstrong and Miguel Indurain, clocked lung capacities of seven and eight litres respectively. Josh joined the British squad in 2001, after leaving Cambridge University. His lungs measured 8.9 litres. Josh was only to hold the title briefly. Pete Reed emerged from Oxford a few years later, in 2004. His lungs caused even more excitement being literally off the chart. The physiologists had to reset the scale on the equipment to record them at more than nine litres. His giant bellows allow him to breathe 220 litres of air in and out every minute whether he is demolishing the rowing machine or the opposition.

So, is it all genetics, Josh?

'I would say this. There are a huge number of physically talented people who never make it because they don't have it upstairs. But, if you don't have the basic physical baseline then you don't even have the chance to make use of mental discipline. Everyone on the start line is genetically well positioned relative to the norm. Of course, you're going to compete against people who are physically potentially superior but you just have to believe they have a mental weakness that you do not have. And that is by and large true because everyone has a mental breaking point.'

So size matters when it comes to lungs and certain aspects of their function are also genetic. Sports scientist and cycling coach Peter Keen worked with British Olympian Chris Boardman. Together they laid the foundations for British sprint cycling success in the last three Olympics. Richard Moore, in his book *Heroes, Villains and Velodromes*, quotes Peter's reaction to testing Chris:

'The guy is completely off the scale in terms of some potentially fundamental characteristics, namely size and function of lungs, which is completely un-trainable; it doesn't change. It's not that he has particularly huge lungs; it's the efficiency with which he can open and close them.'

In fencing, speed and reflexes play a vital role. British fencer Nick Bell could move like lightning – his reflexes were tested in the lab by timing the micro-second lag between a light being switched on and his strike. Granted, he was being tested after many years of fencing training and not before he picked up a foil at the start of his career, which would better measure his innate genetic talent, but I'll bet within a few years scientists will have unearthed a number of genetic links to reflex speed and, potentially, speed of nerve impulse. Nick's reflexes and speed, together with his long arms and ability to curve his body almost into a concave C shape (making striking his body almost impossible), help to make a champion. Plus he's left-handed.

'If you go to the top level of fencing I'd say it is 40:60 lefties.' This is far above average. In the population as a whole, 10 to 15 per cent are left-handed. While still contentious, it is believed that hand preference is produced by genetic causes.

'I put it [the high ratio of lefties at the top] down to natural selection at an early age. When you're in the novices, if you're left-handed you will have an advantage. But once you get to the top level it's a bit like tennis, it doesn't really make a difference [to the outcome].'

In May 2011, a US company AIBioTech, released a mail order genetic testing kit labelled the Sports X Factor. The kit tests eight genetic markers to help customers assess which sports they could excel in. For just a few hundred dollars pushy parents can discover which sport they should channel their children into. Top of the bill, the test for the so-called 'speed gene', ACTN3. ACTN3 provides genetic instructions for a specific muscle protein, important in explosive sports like weight-lifting and sprinting. If you haven't got a working copy of the gene, you're extremely unlikely to be an Olympian level sprinter. About 82 per cent of the general populous have at least one working copy of the ACTN3 gene, whereas more than 97 per cent of Olympic sprinters have at least one copy.

And we're still really only at the beginnings of the young field of sports genetics. So maybe it is all in the genes?

Practice, practice, practice

In Atlanta 1996, Great Britain finished a disastrous 36th in the medal table, behind such sporting titans as Algeria, Kazakhstan and North Korea. Britain's greatest Olympian, Sir Steven Redgrave, and his super-lunged partner Matthew Pinsent, won Britain's only gold medal. A paltry eight silver and six bronze medals made up the rest of the haul.

Four years later, in Sydney, the now re-branded Team GB, rocketed to 10th in the medal table. A much more respectable 11 gold medals, 10 silvers and seven bronze. Suddenly we were holding our own. OK, Holland and Cuba were still ahead marginally in eighth and ninth, with populations less than a quarter our size, but at least we'd put Algeria well behind us. It was our biggest haul of gold medals since 1920.

Athens proved Sydney was no fluke, with Team GB again 10th in the medal standings, bagging 31 medals. In Beijing the team exceeded even their own, now pretty lofty, expectations to finish fourth in the rankings – behind the giants China, Russia and the USA.

Having been the lame duck of international sport in Atlanta, the British team has become a real force to be reckoned with. Within the team itself a strong sense of confidence developed and with it an unashamed expectation of putting in medal quality performances. Other country's athletes have learnt the hard way to respect the quality of British athletes. In some sports this extends even further, to a sense of awe, almost fear. Suddenly, in sports like cycling, sailing and rowing, the plucky Brits, previously the gallant losers, have become the country to beat.

What happened to the British team in a little over a decade, between the dark days of Atlanta and a single gold at Lake Lanier to mixing it with superpowers? Such a consistent and broad improvement can't be down to a run of good luck. A new generation of genetically vastly improved athletes? Impossible in just four years between Atlanta and Sydney. Did a British team physiologist discover an undetectable new performance-enhancing drug – or variety of drugs – to systematically supercharge Team GB? Perhaps the next generation of The Clear? Well, if there was a Clear Mk. 2 doing the rounds I was never offered it, besides, Team GB's sudden success was so broad that no single drug could have boosted performance across such a variety of sports like sailing, cycling and eventing. What then?

That most unlikely saviour: a government quango.

The year following the dismal performance in Atlanta, UK Sport was established in London to save Britain's blushes. Its remit? To lift the performance of Britain's elite athletes and drag us up from the dregs of the medal table with multi-million pound investment. Since 2006, and the award of the Olympics to London, the resources behind UK Sport have grown further, with the Government promising an additional

£300m for high performance sport up to 2012. Today, UK Sport's 90 staff invest around £100m a year from Lottery and Government funds to support 1,200 of our best athletes. That equates to £83k per elite athlete, most of which funds a world class support structure, the best coaches, psychologists, physiotherapists, dieticians and staff in the world. It also provides for great equipment and fully funded overseas and altitude training camps.

Most importantly, around a quarter of that funding goes direct to athletes. Overnight Britain's best athletes became professionals. Suddenly we could train all day, every day. No longer were we amateurs, fitting in training before or after work. For the four years prior to my lottery funding I'd been training with some of the best coaches in the world, and with superb equipment and support but only for 18 hours or so a week (about two sessions a day, the first at an un-sociable 6am). After four years of that I managed to break into the British team and medal at the World Championships. The next year, now on the National Lottery's tab, I could train 32 hours a week. My performance leapt. Personal bests dropped. On the key physiological test I was 1.6 per cent faster. That may not sound like much but as you near the top of sport the parabola of performance improvement begins to level out and the differences between the medallists and the also-rans are measured in fractions of a per cent. That 1.6 per cent lifted me to a different level.

And Lottery funding suddenly gave team managers a huge amount of control over their athletes. They could decide where the athletes should live, who they should be coached by and which events they should compete at. If you don't play ball the funding can be withdrawn. Olympic level performances are needed at each national trial. Have a bad race and the lifeline could be abruptly stopped. The athletes resent being so tightly controlled but it sure works.

Three weeks after my first World Championship medal, on a pre-season cross training camp, I had 'the chat' with the Godfather-like team manager. He confirmed he'd been able to secure me a UK Sport National Lottery Grant, a B level grant to be exact; £22k tax free and with a few thousand pounds of equipment allowance. I clenched my fist in victory under the table and tried not to give away my relief. I'd been half expecting a C level grant – £12k doesn't go very far. He made it clear he'd had to work hard to secure it for me and that the funding would be kept under review through the year. I was under no illusions. From that moment on I was his. I trained where and when he directed, followed the head coach's training programme to the letter, ate what they told me and went to every trial and race. It was no surprise when at national trials later that year the fastest nine performers were all Lottery funded.

The National Lottery funding allows athletes to clock up Gladwell's and Syed's magic 10,000 hours of practice much more rapidly and still within the right age bracket for peak performance. I started intense training in my sport aged 15. By the time I'd left school I had more than 2,000 hours under my belt. Through university I was clocking about 800 hours a year of training time, excluding the same amount again of travel time, washing, eating. On the Lottery's tab I could double that to 1,600 or so hours a year. By the opening ceremony of the Athens Games I'd put in almost exactly 7,000 hours of training in the sport. Damn it. Only needed another 3,000.

For some sports you couldn't even have got to the start line without serious funding. I asked Sian Brice what difference it made to her.

'It made all the difference really. In '98 I was one of the first people to get Lottery funding. It was nowhere near as much as I was getting working at the bank but I knew if I wanted to progress I'd have to go professional. I feel so lucky to have been a part of it at the start of Lottery funding when there was quite a bit of money around. We had access to all these amazing coaches suddenly, like Robin Broom the Olympic swimming coach.

'You couldn't even have qualified without [the Lottery]. The World Cup races are all over the world. They start in Australia and Japan in April, then come back to Europe for May, June, July, then go over to America and Mexico in September and back to Australia for the end of the season. It's a big circuit and a very expensive business. You couldn't even have got to the races to qualify without the funding.

'And other countries were getting funded, like the Australians, through their National Institute of Sport. Apparently Spain had the most amazing system. France the same – they were all based in Paris with their performance director, they all had funding, all travelled. So nearly every country – Japan, America – they all had a similar kind of professional set up. You're nowhere if you don't.'

The day of the amateur Olympian is over. In fact, it's been over for decades. Susie Murphy was fencing against professionals in Mexico, Munich and Montreal.

'It started with the Iron Curtain countries in the 1960s. Anybody who showed any talent, whether it be gymnastics or fencing or whatever, they were sent to the academy in Moscow. And there they were trained, full time. They arrived at an Olympics or World Championships fine-tuned, hitting their peak at the right time. Whereas we rocked up, having been working during the day, training in the evenings, maybe with a training weekend in Aldershot where we lifted a few medicine balls, and it's hit or miss. Back then, in 1968, we were so naive. And it was daunting going up against them. We knew we were underdogs. Professionals against amateurs. My very first fight in my pool was against the Russian fencer Elena Novikova. It was David versus Goliath. She was about 6'1". Quite clearly she thought, well I've got a Brit, I'm OK here.'

Susie lost. But only just. 4–3.

'She learned not to underestimate a Brit again, especially when they're a foot shorter that you. She went on to win the gold medal.' The first of Novikova's six Olympic medals. Susie wistfully concluded, 'I just wish I was competing now, because the strategy that goes behind creating a good fencer is totally different. Then it was just so naive.'

Nick Bell also went foil to foil with professionals in the 1970s and '80s.

'The big nations were the Italians, Germans, French (the French were ten times better than the English!) and all the Eastern European bloc – Russians, Hungarians, Poles. They were all professional, don't believe anything else. Many were either in the army or PE teachers with dispensation to train full time. The Eastern Bloc fencers would earn extra money trafficking caviar, vodka and Cuban cigars across the border in their fencing bags. On the way back their bags would be full of instant coffee, nylon stockings and hard currency. They'd even sell their fencing kit in the West to make room for more goods. That's what motivated Boris Onishchenko in Montreal, the pentathlon fencer.'

Boris Onishchenko was an extremely successful professional, nominally an army officer from the Ukraine, whose career ended in ignominy.

'He was already modern pentathlon Olympic medallist three times over, so he didn't need to prove anything. He just wanted to hang on in there so he could keep up trading, hence the cheating thing against Steve Fox. It was the highlight of that Games! Normally you have two wires up an epee to the point and when you strike it makes electrical contact and the light comes on. But he had two other little wires in his handle and a button in his sword.'

Boris's sword could trigger the electronic scoring system at will. Jim Fox of the British team protested that Onishchenko was managing to score without hitting him. Officials replaced Onishchenko's sword and discovered the extra wiring. The British went on to the gold while Boris earned the label 'Disonischenko' in the press and the enmity of the Soviet team; the USSR volleyball team reportedly threatening to throw him out of a hotel window. The irony is that Boris may well have won without the extra electrics. Even without cheating, wherever there is professionalism there is victory. Just look at the top of the Beijing medal table.

China established a vast national and regionally-funded athlete recruitment and funding programme before their Olympics. In Russia, a mix of public funding and private sponsorship funds the athletes. Holland punched far above its weight, placing twelfth with a population of only 16 million, thanks in significant part to the Lotto funding of the Dutch Olympic Committee, which in turn funds the different sporting federations. The Australian Olympic Committee funds national sporting bodies, coaches and athletes from sponsorship and licensing deals, AOC fundraising, state funding and IOC grants. Like the UK's National Lottery funded UK Sport, The Australian Institute of Sport was set up in 1980 after an Atlanta-style debacle, with Australia coming 32nd in the medal table in Montreal 1976, without a single gold. An Olympian from France, which just made the top 10 in Beijing, told me, 'Most of the funding comes from the State. The Ministry of Sport provides funding to the different federations but it is barely enough to survive. So federations often conclude partnerships with private companies, who hire athletes on part-time jobs paid as full.'

The USA, the spiritual home of capitalism, takes it further and is one of only a handful of countries where there is no government funding of the Olympic team. The US Olympic Committee relies on the sale of television broadcast rights and corporate sponsorship. Private companies in the US have been playing their part through the Olympic Job Opportunities Programme (OJOP) for decades. One US Olympian of the 1980s gave a flavour of how it worked.

'I worked in a bank – Wells Fargo – I was the only guy at the bank who actually kept bankers' hours, back then 10 till 3. They had a programme where they took on a few athletes who were trying out for the Olympics. I was one of the fortunate ones. I actually had a job that got me a few bucks. They were very generous but God knows I had to spend every penny of it and a lot more [on my sport]. If I'd had half a brain at the time, I'd have stayed at Wells Fargo. I'd be on an island near Tahiti right now. I used to train at 6.30am and work out for two and a half hours and then do another work-out after work. We thought we were professionals, but today they're really professionals. Little did I know you could work even harder. If you win the Games you get a chunk of money too, maybe $40k.'

Even further down the medal table you find professionals. The Pakistani marksman in Beijing, Siddiq Umar, nominally serves in Pakistan's army. The Kenyan Athletic Association is government funded, with an Olympic budget of around $1.5 million.

It is often said that when Olympians get to the start line they've all done similar amounts of training. This simply isn't true, even professionals differ in the time and intensity of their training. Here's Sian Brice again.

'I trained hard but the triathletes under Brett Sutton did training that nobody else would comprehend. He's trained a lot of World Champions and Olympians at his base in Switzerland. They do unbelievably hard training. He's produced so many World Champions, like Chrissy Wellington and Loretta Harrop, who should have won gold in Athens. Before a normal World Cup race [Loretta] would go for a two hour run in the morning – a two hour run before the race when we were all resting up for three days beforehand. She was a black belt in judo and hard as nails. Sutton's theory is that you make people train harder than they believe possible. If they're not broken by the training he'd make them so tough, mentally and physically, and in races they'd know they had trained ten times harder than anybody. The international circuit had two World Cup events in Japan with a week between them when we would all do a little bit of training but short, sharp sessions. In the middle of the week between World Cup races Sutton would have his athletes do 60 x 400m. At pace. A normal session for me, when I was training hard would be 15 x 400m. He would flog 100 people but make two World Champions, normally a man and woman each year from his stable.'

Professionalism equals practice, lots of it. But not all practice is equal. Maybe Matthew Syed is right; we can all be great if we put in the required amount of intense training into our chosen pursuits.

Something in the human psyche draws us to making straightforward answers to difficult and broad questions. We want to believe there are a few simple traits that set apart the greats from the average, that everyone has a USP. I'm sorry to disappoint. Matthew, it's far more than just practice. Watson and Crick, we are far more than our genetic blueprint. There are not just mental factors, like motivation and psychological strength, that play a role but also lots of luck. Like answering a simple question with a complex answer, putting outcomes down to chance, fate or randomness is traditionally unpopular. We like a solid rationale we can try to control. Another self-help book yet to hit the bestseller list is *It's All Down to Luck So Just Cross Your Fingers*.

Here's one bronze medallist.

'I think luck plays a far bigger part than anybody would dare to believe. Everybody at that level trains really hard, everybody thinks that they're doing that extra session on Christmas Day but actually everybody else is doing that same extra session so you don't gain anything. Everybody turns up to the Olympics thinking that they're in the best shape of their lives. I really think that luck plays a part in what goes on in so many ways. There are so many things that can go right and can go wrong.

'You prepare so hard and plan for every eventuality, you know exactly what you're doing for the final week in the run up, the day before, the warm-up, the race. It can feel like everything just comes off like you're reading a book because you know exactly what you're doing. But there are some things that are out of your control and that is where the luck comes in. Stuff like illness can just jump out.'

There are obvious spots of bad luck, such as the gold medal favourite randomly catching a virus the day before the final. Some might also call the fumbling of a baton in a sprint relay or a foot fault in the long jump luck. Then there is pure randomness. In Athens, Brazilian marathon runner Vanderlei de Lima was leading the race with 10km to go until former priest and religious zealot Cornelius Horan bundled him off the road to publicise the second coming. Lima escaped to take bronze and eventually received the Pierre de Coubertin medal for sportsmanship but he would surely rather be Olympic champion.

Nick Bell remembered the '76 and '84 winners from his foil event. 'They had this incredible belief in themselves. But in 1984 it went to nine all and it could easily have been the German who got that last hit.

It was all down to the last hit. A three hundredth of a second strike and it's all over. One's a gold medallist, the other a silver medallist but you only remember the winner.' In retrospect the eventual victor looks predestined, but of course it's not.

In addition to acts of God and micro-second randomness, there is 'big picture luck' which is harder to discern. Steve Batchelor recounted how the Russian boycott of the '84 Olympics allowed his previously unqualified team to sneak a surprise bronze, which provided the platform for gold in Seoul. To quote Steve, 'Now that's what I call luck.' British cycling had the great fortune of Chris Hoy being born and raised in Edinburgh, the only Scottish city with a velodrome, admittedly a roofless one. Gold medallist rower Tom James similarly recognised the fortune of his own upbringing.

'I've been lucky enough to find a sport which suits my genetics. I'd be awful at the 100m or the high jump. I can't sprint to save my life, so sports like tennis or football are out, whereas rowing suits my physiology. I've got big lungs, long arms. A long back, which isn't great, and short legs (I'd love to have slightly longer legs), but I've got a VO_2 max of 6.7 litres which is third highest in the squad. I was lucky to find rowing at school.'

And Tom recognised luck later in his career. 'If Tom Parker hadn't got ill before the World Championships in 2007, I wouldn't have got in the bow seat of the eight and got a bronze medal. So then I wouldn't have got such a good pairs partner and it's likely I wouldn't have come second in all those trials and been in a position to be allowed to seat race [for the top boat]. Now, I could have got there another route but that gave me a lot of leg ups. I might not be a gold medallist today if Tom Parker hadn't got a stomach bug in Munich.'

Most athletes don't like the thought of anything being out of their control or being random. One Beijing medallist strongly disagreed when I suggested that luck plays a role.

'I wouldn't call it luck. Part of being a great sportsman is being able to take best advantage of circumstance. That often looks like luck, but there is a skill to that as well. You can be handed an awesome deck of cards and screw it up – or be handed a mediocre deck of cards and play it really well. Success is about seizing opportunities. I remember the GB 4 x 100m team in Athens. They weren't the best four sprinters but they were totally primed to take advantage of the moment. That was quite an important thing to see. You train the whole time to put in your best performance so that you're ready to seize an opportunity.'

So you need genetics, practice and the right sort of luck. But it's all for nothing if an athlete doesn't have it upstairs. Firstly, motivation. All the athletes you see at the Olympics are survivors. Out of thousands who started their sport, the Olympians kept at it long after most of their vintage have given up. As a Beijing silver medallist said to me, 'Keep going long enough and the guys that used to beat you, give up.'

It's not the world's best possible physical specimens at the Olympics, it's the world's best specimens that had the hunger and drive to keep going. I knew plenty of guys who had much greater potential than I did, who quit after leaving school.

Steve Batchelor articulates the loss of talent through the years in hockey. 'When I was playing U16s there used to be a guy called Nigel Stevenson who was captain of the U16 British Team. I used to think he was unbelievable, superb. A brilliant, amazing player. But he didn't make the step up to U18s. And there was a whole load of U18s who didn't make it up to U21s. Then from U21s very few make it to the next stage up.'

You've got to have the fire inside to keep at it to eventually make it. Fencer Nick Bell fenced his best whilst going through an unhappy divorce and a fight over his children.

'In 1991, three days after the World Champs, we fought the Austrians for an Olympic qualification spot and I just annihilated the Austrian team. Their star had just come third in the World Championships and I beat him 5–0. After that my divorce came through and I got custody of my children and suddenly all the anger and focus had gone. I went into the 1992 season doing the circuit but I ended up being dropped from the team. I just didn't have the same motivation. It was an interesting insight into focus and what makes you do things – I hadn't lost my skills at all, just the mindset.'

An American gold medallist gave me his analysis on the mentality needed: 'You need to be born with seven to nine loose screws in your psyche to be a champion. But lots of guys have seven to nine loose screws ... maybe 3 per cent of the population. Take those screws and use them to apply yourself body-and-soul to being a champion –10,000 hours – it's hard/tedious/boring/fun/challenging/near impossible for everyone.'

There isn't a one size fits all for the right mental mindset, but it's a crucial ingredient. Here's Tom James again.

'I think mental attitude is very individual. I wouldn't say there is a right mental attitude, I really wouldn't. Intelligence for your sport is overlooked. You know you don't see idiots, people who don't understand themselves or don't understand their sport, getting gold medals. You've got to be clever enough to figure out what works for you and the way you learn, whether it's developing technique or how to use your body to maximise performance, or preparing for a race. Even the trialling process, you've got to understand from a coach's point of view the best way to get selected. I've been labelled a natural but I think what I've done well is I've been very analytical. I feel that I've thought things through and learnt from those around me and the opportunities that I've had. The outcome might then look like a 'natural'. I've sometimes gone into situations being quite scared. It's like, if they only figure it out, they'll easily beat me. They're stronger than me, how can they not? But a lot of the opposition don't think in the right way and when they do analyse performance they don't do it correctly.'

In the final reckoning of what makes those on the podium different, each Olympian has their own, individual take.

A bronze medallist from Athens: 'I think that everybody has the ability – you're capable of training your body to a certain strength and speed and technical ability and all those things. And then it comes down to the mind.'

Sian Brice, 'It's more than just lab results. There are too many variables [for it to be pure physiology]. There's a lot up here [pointing to head]. Triathlon, for example, is really mental because it's an extended event, two hours, so you go through different stages mentally and a lot of decision points.'

Another Olympian threw in her view, a subscriber to professionalism and luck, 'I think it's being super-trained, along with tremendous self will and discipline. What people don't appreciate is the guy who came seventh in that final of the 400m fly and was a split second away from gold. So it's luck on the day. Unless you're an athlete you don't examine it.'

Syed's argument in *Bounce* – train enough and you'll be excellent at whatever you chose – is seductive. It's probably true for table tennis. But in general it's wrong. As Bas van de Goor neatly states, 'You can learn to play volleyball; you can't learn to be tall. Genetics count.' And not just in volleyball. To win the cycling road race you have to have a great lung capacity, maybe not the biggest in the event, but lungs at least big enough. To win the 200m you must have at least one working copy of the ACTN3 gene and a genetic predisposition to a high level of fast twitch muscle. Even in archery or shooting the amount of micro-tremor in the hands can be affected by the levels of thyroxin in the blood (the body's metabolism thermostat effectively), which can be genetically influenced.

If it was all down to practice then sports' governing bodies wouldn't invest in talent ID systems. They'd pick kids at random and train them up. Instead the Australians, British and the Chinese (and the USSR before all of them) run programmes to identify kids with the right potential physiological characteristics. Tom James's latest rowing partner is a product of the British Rowing Team's World Class Start programme, which searches for kids between 16 and 18 who have never rowed before, but have the right strength, height, arm span and endurance characteristics to become Olympic medallists.

Yes, practice is important, but you must want to do 10,000 hours of practice in the first place. Just going through the motions won't cut it. As many Olympians have told me, it was an addiction to their early success that got them hooked, leading them to want to practise more than their compatriots.

I think Olympic Champion Tom James sums up the mix of luck, hard work and talent (genetics) needed to be an Olympian pretty well.

'It's a combination of things. You've got to firstly find the right sport for you, so genetics. Then to an extent the mental side but I think that is overdone. I think everybody has got that ability. I don't feel any different from the average Joe down the street. That can get you to a high standard in your sport. But then to actually win, I think a bit of luck but also you do have to have something that differentiates you a little bit. Whether that's from having done more training than anyone else or something genetically that makes you a little bit better, or having a bit more nous or more intelligence about what you're doing, how you train or how you treat your competition (you know, the face you present to the world, have you won the race before you get to the start line). I think everyone can be great at something. I'm a big believer in that. If you were to give gold, silver and bronze medals to dentists suddenly you'd put those winning medals up on this heroic pedestal. I'm a bit cynical about the Olympics getting put up on this big pedestal. I'm just working through my career like anyone else.'

Bas agreed that winning his gold took the perfect combination of factors, not just genetics. 'We were the biggest team, sure, but with the right amount of experience and young blood, the right mix of personalities and an organisation that was very clear about one thing – anything that doesn't contribute to the ultimate goal has to be eliminated.'

Personally, I believe that innate genetics plays a bigger role than most, but I also recognise that almost none of us reach our physiological potential. The right genes can make some sports a lot more enjoyable through early success and are likely to keep the genetically advantaged in the sport.

One of the discoverers of the Speed Gene, ACTN3, encapsulates the argument. 'This one gene is just a minor ingredient in a large and complex recipe. Super-elite [sprint] athletes need to have the right ACTN3 combination, but they also have to have a whole host of other factors working in their favour.'

Lance Armstrong, who is much better known for his seven consecutive Tour de France victories than his appearances at the Barcelona, Atlanta and Sydney Olympic Games, has had his success analysed more than almost any other athlete. The physiologist Edward Coyle, who runs the Human Performance Lab near Armstrong's home in Austin, Texas, has studied the champion for almost a decade. Lance has a raft of unusual genetic benefits – an oversized heart, vast lungs for his size, a body that produces about half the normal levels of lactic acid and the most efficient aerobic system, in terms of oxygen intake to energy released, ever measured – but in Coyle's view that's not enough.

'There are about 1,000 people in the US between the ages of 15 and 20 with the same physiological potential, but none of them will achieve what he has without the training and the daring of Lance.' That and a large dose of luck.

CHAPTER 7

the release

Into temptation

St Catherine's School, Kifissia, Athens
20 August 2004 18.45pm

'Free beer starts in 15 minutes!' A slurred cheer goes up. The six of us chink our paid-for beers in celebration; three of us Olympic athletes, one girlfriend and two of her friends, who giggle drunkenly.

Poolside at the British team lodge has become the 'pre-game' warm-up before the night really begins. The BOA has hired a school, St Catherine's British School, Kifissia, as a private get away for British athletes, support staff and their friends and family. They've created a team lodge at each Games since Barcelona apparently.

Fifteen minutes away from the pressures of the Village, during the day it provides a quiet, private place of solace for the athletes still in competition to meet their parents and loved ones, as getting guests into the Village is pretty much impossible. There's free food, soft drinks (English breakfast tea!), British newspapers and a large TV with the BBC footage. Even Team GB bean bags. British athletes' results and timings for forthcoming competitions are posted across one huge wall. Union Jack bunting is everywhere.

Most of the in-competition athletes tend to gravitate to the shaded tables round the pool, away from the blare of the BBC commentary and the wall chart of medallists. The last time I was here in the afternoon I saw the 17-year-old boxer Amir Khan reduced to a grumpy teenager with his Mum fussing around him. And he looks so cocky and confident in the ring. Paula Radcliffe was two tables away, sitting with her husband (and coach), visibly trying to relax – and failing. She's carrying the pressure with her everywhere. We all know she's more than good enough to win. That just makes it worse.

'So, where tonight then?' An important and difficult question – with our Olympic kit and medallist mates we can get into any party in the city. And be the centre of attention. With only a handful of party nights at an Olympics as an athlete you can't afford to pick a single dud bash.

'Let's do the Dutch House to start, good DJ tonight,' Rob chips in.

'And more free beer,' Jamie grins, lifting his bottle in salute. The Dutch House's official name is the Heineken House.

We start on a few drinking games and after a few rounds of fives and 'I have never … ' we move inside to watch the athletics on the Beeb. Jamie pours drinks, having flirted his way behind the bar. I reflect that I'm managing to ignore the questions deeper within very successfully. I'll have the rest of my life to beat myself up over whether I really did push as hard as I could have in racing and, in a few months I'll have to decide whether to roll the dice again on another four years of sacrifice. Right now, losing myself in drink, girls and general adoration is proving very easy.

Several hours later I'm at one of the bars of the Heineken House talking to the Wolf, an American with cool facial hair, who was last in his Olympic final yesterday, having been World Champion the year before. Shattering, particularly for a previous World Champion, but he's already decided to give it another four years.

'What are you doing tomorrow, man?' he shouts across to me while we wait for our drinks. Euphoric house music thumps at chest-shaking volume.

'Cheering on our girls in the morning,' I'm interrupted by a blonde Dutch girl handing us our Heinekens. She's got the T-shirt and badge of a volunteer and has Dutch flags painted on her cheeks. We turn to the crowd with our drinks and I continue, 'Then I'm picking up my girlfriend and watching the marathon.'

Wolf frowns sternly, knitting his thick, dark eyebrows. 'You brought your girlfriend here?' incredulously, jabbing a thumb in the direction of the dance floor. 'Man,' he sighs, shaking his head, 'that's like bringing sand to the beach.'

Clearly disappointed with me, Wolf heads off into the crowd, a sea of bright orange shirts. Cheery Dutch everywhere. Their love of a good party, ability to each speak about eight languages and the affordable beer has attracted lots of other European Olympians and their friends.

The music quietens briefly to allow another of today's Dutch medallists to be announced onto the stage. They come out to rapturous cheering and the visibly overwhelmed guy waves happily. DJ Tiesto launches into more ear-splitting trance. The Olympian is beckoned to crowd surf off the stage. Up above the dance floor, on a gantry, I can see a reporter talking into a camera animatedly. The Acropolis is lit up on the hill behind him.

I head back through the crowd to find another mate on the Dutch team. He's chatting to an Aussie athlete so I strike up a conversation with his wife. We chat about what sports we're going to see in the next few days and how our teams are faring thus far. Then she says matter-of-factly, 'By the way, which would you prefer, blonde or brunette?' Behind her half a dozen girls from her university are chatting excitedly. Lithe, sporty and happily drunk, the Dutch students are eyeing me with unabashed interest, having noted my Team GB polo shirt.

I look to the ceiling to search for inner strength. Tonight is going to require a Herculean effort of self-control.

The unintentional pick-up artists at the ultimate party

Imagine if you had a magic wand which meant you could go anywhere in the city, jump any queue, be universally adored and have everyone throw themselves at you. A wand which makes bouncers beckon you smiling into nightclubs, lifting the cordon and waving you and your many friends and hangers-on through. In a club or bar you never have to buy a drink, not one. It's impossible. Everyone wants to talk to you, buy you a drink or just be seen with you. Members of the opposite sex approach and try desperately to get you into bed.

That's pretty much what it's like when you have an Olympic medal round your neck. Even non-medallists enjoy 95 per cent of the magical aphrodisiac effect. For Olympians who've been cooped up monk-like on training camps for months, it is sensory overload.

A few months after Athens I understood more clearly why the Olympian effect is quite so potent. Sitting next to a friend on a plane to a wedding I was woken by his occasional guffaws. He was avidly reading and scribbling notes on *The Game* – a book about picking up members of the opposite sex. Reading his scribbled notes it struck me that Olympians are unwittingly following some of *The Game*'s top recommendations.

- Peacocking – like the resplendent bird, this is all about dressing to be noticed, with attention-grabbing clothes which provide ammunition for an ice-breaking conversation. Rather than a loud shirt or a piece of interesting jewellery, during the Games off-duty Olympians are generally seen out in national team polo shirts. These are typically pretty colourful items, embossed with flags and insignias, providing ample excuse for anyone wanting to talk to you to approach and ask what sport you competed in. And everyone has their names on their accreditation swinging round their necks which helps break the ice.
- Showing worth – being good at something is sexy, being really good at something extremely so. Being an Olympian proves you've got some of the best genes in the gene pool. Having initiated communications through successful peacocking, during the ensuing conversation the pick-up artist will 'prove their worth' by steering the conversation, intentionally or otherwise, onto a topic which highlights their great skill at something. Olympians prove their worth very easily, inevitably in the first few lines of conversation, responding to the questions posed to them which come in this order. 1. What did you compete in? 2. Did you get a medal?

- Confidence, confidence, confidence – throughout the whirlwind of peacocking, proving worth and flirting, complete self-confidence is required. Partying Olympians are bubbling with confidence – not only does everyone want to talk to them, laugh at their jokes and hang on their every word, but the Olympians have been working on their self-confidence for months, if not years, with trained psychologists.

Together it's a powerful mix and even normally shy and retiring Olympians can have a lot of fun, particularly as boyfriends and girlfriends lack the accreditations, medals and free passes to access all areas, so are often out of the picture.

It's not just the Olympic aphrodisiac effect that results in disreputable goings on. There is a perfect storm of factors which makes the Olympics not just the greatest show on earth but the best party destination on the planet.

Olympians have serious motivation to party hard. All have sacrificed innumerable hen parties, stag weekends, weddings, birthdays and other opportunities for merriment, instead spending their time going to bed early, on training camp or just being exhausted. They are overdue some raving. Then their Olympic results super-charge their merry-making further. Each is either on cloud nine, having exceeded their expectations and perhaps medalled, or they are on a one-way trip to self-destruction and obliteration, losing themselves in free drink and illicit liaisons, having not achieved what they so desperately hoped and worked for. The latter creates some unlikely pairings. An American athlete who had a disappointing Barcelona and would later go on to great things is rumoured to have ended up in bed the night of his race with a capacious European woman rower. In his biography the day is down as the worst in his life. The sizeable bedmate isn't mentioned.

The thousands of others in the Olympic city – friends and family of athletes, tourists, off-duty officials, volunteers and locals are also determined to make it a fortnight worth remembering. Most are on foreign soil which releases inhibitions further and allows them to do things they simply wouldn't on home turf. A 'what goes on tour, stays on tour' mentality takes hold across the entire city.

The athletes have the physical capacity to really go for it all night long. These are the fittest members of the human race, so dancing until dawn isn't a problem. No need for time-outs or taking a breather. Two Beijing silver medallists I spoke to didn't get back to their Village digs before 7am for the entire week after their Olympic final. Now that's endurance.

Booze can be the stumbling block. Almost all the Olympians have a pathetic alcohol tolerance, relative to their size, after months of hard training (although the French Olympian from Athens put his drunkenness squarely down to the Greek wine in Athens). Many have been on complete drinking bans for months. Speaking to Steve Batchelor the British hockey team didn't touch a drop of alcohol for three months before Seoul. Moving from abstinence to excess results in casualties along the way each evening but being ultra-fit most deal with hangovers and lack of sleep well, the highly tuned bodies just clear the alcohol rather than the lactic acid. Memories of these ultimate events can be unfortunately vague (from the perspective of one writing about them). Asking one Athens Olympian about the partying after his event revealed this less-than-juicy titbit. 'It's all pretty hazy. I honestly remember so little.'

Mixed into the recipe for Olympic revelry, along with super-fit athletes, a crowd determined to have a good time and the sexiness of Olympic greatness, millions of marketing dollars are spent by brands in creating the backdrop for amazing parties.

Talking to Olympians of different eras, each Olympics seems to have a defining party. Those at Athens still talk about the *Sports Illustrated* event. A British bronze medallist reports, 'There were legends of our time, legends from previous Olympics and absolute superstars. Everybody who was anybody in the sports world. American basketball players, track and field stars, Carl Lewis and that kind of thing. The food was amazing and by now we're allowed to eat it and drink it.'

Here's another British medallist's recollection. 'It was awesome. You had topless dancers. The US synchronised swimming team doing their thing in the pool. Amazing food.' He also remembers bumping into Evander Holyfield and the exciting opportunity to chat to swimsuit models.

He then watched one of his taller British teammates sidle up to an Australian competitor and good friend of his. The Australian was deep in conversation with an American swimsuit model. The cheery Brit lifted his beer to 'cheers' the Aussie and in his exuberance shattered both glasses and covered the model with broken glass and beer. Not half an hour later the good-looking Aussie was in earnest focused discussion with another attractive blonde, the previous one having had to leave to get changed. His lanky Brit friend spied him across the room again, walked up, tripped over a stool and fell flat on his face in front of the couple. The Brit gathered himself up with blood gushing down his leg and put his arm round the unimpressed looking Australian.

The Aussie flatly denied all knowledge of the drunken Brit to the swimsuit model. 'I don't know this man.'

The loveable drunken Brit, sweetly replied, 'Mike, what do you mean?' The second model of the night drifted away from the Antipodean after the Brit went for a team hug but he did eventually succeed in his quest. Third time lucky.

Most of the major teams now create a team lodge at each Games. For 2012, the Germans hired the Museum of London, Docklands to be the 'Deutsches Haus'; the Brazilians hired Somerset House; the Italians took the QE2 conference centre in Westminster; the Chinese selected Richmond, near their training venue (partying clearly low on the agenda); and the Dutch took Alexandra Palace as the location of the Heineken House (Heineken once again being a sponsor of the Olympics following their c. $50m sponsorship of Athens).

In Beijing, Budweiser made their sponsorship of the Games 'experiential' and created Club Bud, also known as The American House, which was the place to be. Close to the bars of the Sanlitun district (where Corona was also sponsoring a few bars – lots of sombreros and inflatable Corero beer bottles) and down the road from the Hard Rock Café, the giant Club Bud venue was difficult to miss. Walking up the long entranceway, excited party-goers of different nationalities gazed up at the roving search lights which lit up the night sky and the 20ft-high illuminated Budweiser sign on the rooftop. The barricaded red carpet walkway, which led to a raised stage for paparazzi-style photos before entry through a giant circular door, made everyone feel like a gold medallist regardless of result.

Inside, Chinese dancers and acrobats spun and whirled streamers while former heavyweight boxing champions posed amiably for photos, one resplendent with top hat and cane. The night I was there the external bar/club area was particularly popular. Free Bud for all at the bar of course, specially installed swimming pool, fake grass, cabanas and Chinese lanterns which threaded across the sky. The buzz at the party that night was all about the US swim team and multi-gold medal winner Michael Phelps potentially coming along later after his final event, maybe even for a 'swim-off' in the pool against the Thorpedo. To my discredit I can't remember whether Phelps did turn up. Too many Buds. Researching Club Bud further after the Games it turns out Budweiser had hired the Chinese National Agricultural Exhibition centre which provided 3,600 square metres of partying space and held 2,000 people at its themed parties. The party schedule kicked off with an MTV China night, then worked its way through the Feng Shui elements (I think I must have been at the fire event – I remember lots of fire breathing going on) and wrapped up with a gold medal celebration night.

In Sydney, the party scene was predictably down by the harbour at various clubs, where previous medallists-turned-commentators like Michael Johnson were to be seen mixing it with the latest crop. A first-time British Olympian remembers, 'It was a revelation that there could be so many parties and everything was free. There was this tiny club called Youth Club, like 150 people or something. Every night there would be a different band playing, they had all the bands that played in the opening and closing ceremonies. There was a whole mix of sports and a lot of Australians and all the Aussie superstars, like the Thorpedo.'

In Atlanta, the chilled out poolside vibe and free sunglasses of the Oakley House made it a popular evening hang out, before the crowd moved on to the nightclub district later on each night. After Mexico half the Olympians went down to party in Acapulco. Barcelona was about the fantastic beach-side scene, as was Los Angeles, although an LA Olympian confessed the Americans added a novel touch. 'We had these curvy hostesses who drove us round in these cars. There was all sorts of … eye opening stuff. I had a good time on all fronts.'

Perhaps the most poignant party was held in Munich 1972, the Olympics where 11 Israeli athletes were killed following their abduction from the Village by the Palestinian terrorist group Black September. Following the closing ceremony, the athletes returned to the Village and converged on the discotheque. John Lennon's 'Give Peace a Chance' was played several times with its poignant relevance. Fencer Susie Murphy's overriding memory of Munich was a touchingly united scene with athletes of all nations singing along to Lennon in one unified voice, arms round each other's shoulders, in defiance of the atrocity.

Village people (part 2)

During the Games the Olympic Village performs a gradual metamorphosis from monastery to Club 18–30. The icy chilled bins of Powerade are increasingly raided as hangover medicine rather than as part of pre-competition 'hydration strategies'. More and more, athletes from competing nations can be seen casually chatting to each other in the Village square or internet cafés. There is time for friendships, perhaps with competitors of many years or teammates from different sports. There is time for flirting too as the electrified atmosphere generated by thousands of psyched athletes seeps away to be replaced by crackling sexual tension.

The vast food hall may be big enough to feed the 5,000 and provides thousands of different foods to cater for the 200 or so competing nations, but at 7am after a big night out, the post-competition athletes accumulate at McDonald's (the only branded food outlet thanks to their sponsorship). A Beijing Olympian lamented, 'It was really quite sad seeing so many people around McDonald's.'

Maurice Greene, the American sprinter, was even spotted in Athens enjoying a Big Mac, outside the Village, clearly feeling flush from his endorsements. The day before his 4 x 100m final. In fairness he'd already won the 100m a few days before. And his team won the relay too anyway despite his burger naughtiness.

The slot your sport has in the Olympic programme seriously affects your Olympic experience and recollections – how much time you spend in the monastery versus party nirvana. Steve Batchelor saw more of the monastery in 1984 than he'd have liked. 'The first sport to finish in the Olympics is the cycling road race. They're finished day one and that's it. Hockey on the other hand lasts the full two weeks.' At least if you're lucky enough to win a gold medal like Steve's team, who spent the day following their match watching it replayed in the Village video room cheering at themselves.

'As you go through the Games, the Village gets noisier and noisier. There are more and more people with bugger all to do and they're not going to leave the Olympic Village. It's like a free holiday for two weeks just waiting for the closing ceremony. And we were there trying to concentrate!'

Nick Bell, on the foil team, picked the right sport I think. 'In fencing you've got foil, epee and sabre. The foilists always had the best deal. We were always on first and the epeeists were always on last. So the epee-ists came out at the same time as us, a few weeks before the Games, and would have four weeks before they started. By the time they started they would be getting a bit jaded. Whereas for us the first event was the men's individual foil, then three days later the men's team foil – so after seven or eight days we were done, yeah! It was party time! And you could really enjoy the Games. We were very lucky. Choosing the foil is the right way to go.'

If I were ultra-talented and could pick my Olympic sport (rather than having it choose me), I'd opt for one finishing in the middle of the Games, like the 50m rifle shoot or the men's 85kg weight-lifting. It's not all over in an anti-climactic flash with the opening ceremony music still ringing in your ears. You get to watch a few days of other events (on TV), see other athletes have their dreams come true or be shattered and get an appreciation of what the Olympics is all about. Sure, the pressure is horrific but with retrospect that's all part of the experience. With an event right at the end of the schedule, like the marathon, by the time you finally get there almost all of your compatriots in the Village are thinking about other things (or have horrific hangovers and are unable to think) and you're the only one spoiling the party. Then you race – and everyone flies home the next day. No chance to decompress, get front row seats to other sports, enjoy your Olympian status at the Games itself or just enjoy the Village.

Life in the Village after competition is simply extremely pleasant. Use that trained psychology to put your result out of your mind (unless you did better than you hoped, in which case revel in that whilst enjoying the surroundings), you have the rest of your life to analyse your performance to death. Lie on the grass and enjoy a free and guilt-free ice cream from one of the many freezer trunks. Enjoy three if you want – you can put the weight on now. Pop to the food hall for any snack you can imagine then pick up some tickets for the athletics that evening. Manage the hangover by dozing through a film in the cinema later on. Post some 'wish you were here' postcards back to domestic rivals at the post office. And just bask in not having Olympic competition, your over-arching goal and overriding concern for the last few years sitting over you, impossible to see beyond. The blindfold and the blinkers have been taken off. You are free. Free of agonising training. Free of having your ears stabbed for their blood three times a day by physiologists. Free of being coached and told what you are doing wrong 100 times a day. Free of having to avoid sun-burn at all costs (it brings blood to the surface of the skin, when it should be in your muscles, as well as making you feel lousy). For now you can relax in the Village. Pop to the art gallery or the shops or the hairdressers or whatever the host nation have put on for you. Enjoy a concert or two from famous local artists. In Barcelona the organisers built a man-made beach. In Vancouver 2010 a computer games room complete with Guitar Hero was installed.

Enjoy the Village as it gradually makes its metamorphosis but abide by the unspoken code of conduct which emerges. The first commandment is:

> Thou shalt not wear medals within the Village walls (although carrying them discreetly on your person is expected to show due respect to your achievement and the aspirations of others)

All the medallists I spoke to confirmed this; Steve Batchelor, hockey gold medallist, sets out why. 'We didn't wear ours around the Village. It's quite difficult, how many athletes win a medal? The other athletes ask to see them, I had mine somewhere on me most of the time but I didn't dare leave it in the apartment. Adrian Moorhouse, the swimmer, got his medal before us. We said well done but none of us went and asked to see it or touch it – we didn't want to jinx our final.'

Medallists take their medals everywhere with them, in the Village and out – everyone they meet wants to look over and feel the inanimate lump of metal and ribbon. A Beijing medallist told me, 'People love to see it. So if you were going shopping you'd show the shop-keeper. If you were going out for a beer you'd show the bar-tender. Anything like that. You'd get money off and it would be fun for everybody. And it helps with girls, clearly.'

The second commandment for life in the Village after your event:

> Thou may party but do not, on pain of death, disturb Olympians still in competition

This is the ultimate and unforgivable faux pas. You can be vomiting drunk and singing merrily only until you're within earshot of in-competition athletes. Disturb their sleep or their mental focus or stretching (quite a few take to stretching on the lawns between apartment blocks) and a black mark of shame is upon you. This rules out parties in Village digs if in-competition athletes are above or below. Far better to take the party outside and sneak back in for a McDonald's as the sun comes up, especially as in theory no alcohol is allowed or served in the Village, although vodka and other drinks get smuggled through security in water bottles.

The winter Olympics of 1998 in Nagano, Japan, saw the American ice hockey team break this sacred commandment and get sent home in disgrace. The NHL (National Hockey League) had specially suspended its league to allow NHL players to attend the Games for the first time. Team USA arrived at the Olympics with great expectations and then proceeded to lose three out of four of their games. Their final game saw them lose to the Czechs and be eliminated from competition by around 5pm. After a degrading press conference ('How can you have lost to amateurs and professionals paid fractions of your salary?') the team was discharged from official duties. Ten hours later a fire extinguisher smashed into the pavement of the Olympic Village having been thrown out of a window five storeys above. Team USA had gone on a rock-and-roll style rampage, concluding by smashing up their dorm rooms and tossing the fire extinguisher out of the window. Lucky no one was hit.

No one likes a bad loser, which this reeked of, even less so when they seem to have had so little regard for others still in competition in the Village. The team was universally condemned, even their own Olympic Committee president stated he was 'deeply disturbed by the behaviour', and they were unceremoniously flown home.

Team USA's conduct also caused a furore about professional athletes competing at the Olympics. 'If they're not going to be appropriately awestruck and treat the Games with respect they should stay at home' was the popular commentary. It's difficult to disagree but for me the

Olympics is not about professional versus amateur. It's about being the pinnacle of the sports it showcases, regardless of whether the sport is commercial enough to support professional athletes. For me, where the Games is not the ultimate Everest in a sport, like tennis or football where Grand Slams and World Cups are of far greater standing, those sports don't belong at the Olympics. The Olympics is about the greats and great exertions – it's not about giving a half-hearted effort, trying to avoid injury and saving yourself for the Premier League in six weeks' time.

The commandment that emerges from day one in Village continues in force:

> Do not pester the megastars for autographs, you are all equals in the Village

After competition things are a little more relaxed so an occasional, very discreet, arms round shoulders photo on an iPhone is just about OK. Fawning, autographs and exclamations of excitement are strict no-nos. As a silver medallist confided, 'There is an etiquette to it, a correct subtle way, after their competition was finished.'

Another must for post-competition athletes is the furthering of international relations through exchanges of kit:

> Be ready to barter, it's rude not to

It is polite, nay expected, to swap some of your vast quantity of sports gear with athletes of other nations. Deals are agreed over lunch in the food hall or at one of the kit trading areas that spring up on the corner of the Village square. Some unwritten rule means no one takes or offers money for kit and no deals are done with non-athletes, you've got to have earned your stripes to be able to trade in them.

With your direct competitors the kit exchange rate is pegged one to one – you must swap something of equal worth with each other but in the wider swapping market exchange rates are quickly established. Australian, American and British gear seems to be rated pretty highly (success being sexy and cool perhaps). German strips are pretty popular too but mostly with non-Europeans. You might, for example, be able to get two Croatian T-shirts, a jumper and leggings for one good Team GB tracksuit top. The smaller Eastern European nations seem to have the weakest currency, although you can pick up some crazily colourful shell suits (e.g. the yellow and turquoise tops of the Ukrainians) which are good for 'gopping kit days' (a bit like mufti day, where on training camp the squad will compete for the most garish outfit). I picked up an astonishing Croatian tracksuit top at a World Championships – soft velour finish, red, yellow, blue stripes radiating from the middle like an LSD sunrise. Probably extremely flammable.

The laws of supply and demand work just as surely in Olympic kit trading as the world's currency markets. Where supply to the market is extremely limited, the price is highest. Cuban Olympic kit is the platinum of international sportswear – extremely rare and highly prized and very difficult to get access to. Minders closely follow the Cuban athletes everywhere, ushering them away from non-Cubans whenever a conversation strikes up, presumably to reduce the risk of defections. The same is true of the Chinese; minders herd their athletes along and away from Westerners, but the large size of the Chinese team versus the small Cuban contingent and the cool retro look of the Cuban gear means it is number one (and in any case finding a Chinese athlete who speaks English to help trade is very difficult). If you manage to find a willing Cuban, separated for a few minutes from his or her minder, this is one situation where money talks, specifically US dollars. It seems the Cuban athletes are not allowed to wear the regalia of other nations back home, rendering it almost valueless, and hard currency is extremely sought after.

In the course of trading it's easy to see which athletes are thinking of retiring, they'll be trading Lycra and leggings for polo shirts, sweat shirts and rucksacks. Always best to leave your favourite gear packed away in your room and never wear something out you wouldn't be comfortable trading to prevent awkward conversations in faltering English along the lines of 'No, I really, really don't want your hideous shell suit top, I wouldn't swap it for a pair of my Olympic briefs'.

Stick to the rules and enjoy the time you have in the Village, it's all too short. Steve Batchelor grinned and stared misty-eyed into the middle distance when giving his recollections of his experiences in Olympic Villages. 'The Village was just the best bit of the Olympics for me, I think. Clearly the competing [is great], you obviously go there trying to do a job and try and win and whatever, but the experiences of the Village and the people you meet and knowing you're part of it. It's just amazing.'

And part of the experience relates to the final commandment. Aside from kit swapping there are other ways of furthering international relations. But remember this:

What happens in the Village, stays in the Village

Deeper, stronger, longer: the sexiest Games ever

As more and more athletes finish their competition, their attention turns to other things. Each other. Cammi Granato, captain of the winning US ice hockey team at the Nagano 1998 winter Olympics (the one not sent away in disgrace) said of the Village:

'It's eye candy all the time. Everybody's checking everybody else out from the moment they get there.'

I haven't met Cammi, I kind of wish I had. I agree with the sentiment. No matter what 'your type' the Olympic Village can cater for it, providing the best physical examples of 'your type' on earth with each of the denizens of the Village having spent years honing their bodies to the needs of their sport. Like men with huge biceps? Go for the canoeists. Tall, lithe women? Volleyball or basketball. Guys built like tanks with a lot to hold onto? Hammer throwers or super heavyweight weight-lifters. Petite little ladies? The gymnasts. It's all there and all on display. The boys and girls of the Village are often dressed in figure-hugging Lycra before competition and are found stretching or limbering up in compromising positions on the grass outside the world's biggest canteen. After competing, they're sunning six-packs with tops off on the grass.

Having completed competition, the athletes need to do something else to burn off their boundless energy. No three-hour training runs or weight-lifting to failure now, like thoroughbred racehorses which haven't had a run out for a while, they get frisky. You can almost smell a fine haze of testosterone and oestrogen wafting through the air. Greatness is sexy, and everyone in the Village is great at something.

No one need know about your indiscretions. The Village is a fenced off little world in a foreign city, behind presidential-style security. Girlfriends, boyfriends or parents are not going to suddenly walk in on you in the act. It couldn't get more different from home so people can do things they'd never normally do. What does all this mean? Sex, and plenty of it, increasing exponentially through the Games as more and more athletes finish competing. And sex means condoms.

The Seoul Games of 1988 saw the first significant distribution of free condoms and the press has been obsessed with the number of condoms provided in the Village ever since. The Albertville Winter Olympics in 1990 saw an escalation in demand, with the condom machines having to be refilled every two hours. With the emergence of AIDS into the international consciousness, by Barcelona in 1992 the authorities distributed between 50,000 and 80,000 condoms (depending on who you ask), to 9,500 athletes. The least sexy modern Games was officially Atlanta: only around 15,000 condoms for 10,500 athletes. In Sydney, 70,000 gold, silver and bronze condoms only lasted the first week, while most athletes were still in a period of relative abstinence before or during competition. The authorities ordered in another 20,000 immediately. Even with this top up, the machines were empty three days before the competition ended. Hot on the heels of Sydney, Salt Lake City in 2002, decided on shock and awe tactics. They announced a plan to distribute 250,000 condoms. After religious groups protested in the Mormon-led city, the Salt Lake organisers caved in and distributed a frugal 100,000 condoms for around 2,500 athletes, comfortably making it the sexiest Olympics ever, with 40 per athlete.

Athens learnt from Sydney. You don't want to run out of condoms mid-Games. The headlines just aren't worth it. So they got in 130,000 condoms – about 13 condoms per athlete. In Beijing the Chinese didn't cut corners: 100,000 condoms were made ready for 16,500 competitors (10,500 in the Village). Each labelled with the inspirational motto, 'faster, higher, stronger' on the wrapping, in both English and Chinese. Some had the 2008 Olympic mascots printed on. Beibei the fish, Jingjing the panda. Nini, the, ahem, swallow… The Chinese didn't stop there, providing another 300,000 condoms and AIDS leaflets to more than 100 city hotels, to keep the Olympic fans in check. There were at least 5,000 of the Village condoms left over (probably the ones with those mood killing mascots on) as a collector(!) called Zhao Xiaokai bought a 5,000 strong lot straight after the Games. The latest winter Olympics, Vancouver 2010, only had a sedate 100,000 distributed, 14 for each of the 7,000 athletes, coaches and officials. Recent Winter Olympics have averaged a rather higher condom/athlete ratio than summer Olympics. Maybe it's the cold.

However, I'm sorry to admit that there isn't quite as much sex as these headline grabbing statistics indicate. In the Village in Athens I got talking to a hockey guy at McDonald's. He'd just been to the loo where he had witnessed some of the Indian team tipping hundreds upon hundreds of condoms into their empty kit bags. Apparently they can sell them back home and make a nice turn. You've got to admire the entrepreneurial spirit. I suspect quite a few nations' athletes take similar advantage of the free condoms. Even early on in the history of free Olympic condom distribution, they weren't being used for their real purpose. The British hockey team went through a huge number as Steve Batchelor reported.

'We were all issued with condoms in Seoul. Everyone went and got them from the doctors for the craic. We made water-bombs out of them and chucked them on people under our tower block in the Village.'

Despite the efforts of entrepreneurs and jokers, there are still a lot of condoms available for their primary purpose, although some types of pairing are a lot more common than others. The ranking of type of sexual liaison is broadly as follows:

1. Same nationality and sport

With plenty of time to have got to know one other on training camps, love or lust can finally blossom with the pressure off and the application of alcohol. As one Olympian winked at me, 'Like murder, it's normally someone you know, which for Olympians means from within your sport.'

Another agreed, 'Certainly within each sport a lot of shenanigans went on, just think of all that testosterone and all these fit, young people thrown together. If you train together and spend a lot of time together, it's an odds on certainty something's going to happen.'

2. Friends and siblings of teammates

A controversial but popular choice. Brothers, sisters and school friends are brought along to parties by Olympians, who naturally introduce them to their teammates, with hilarious consequences (depending on whether it's your sister or not). One recent British team member was persuaded to confess an illicit relationship with a teammate's sister at an Olympic after party. His honesty earned him a swim, fully clothed, and a dripping mobile phone.

3. Other sports within the same national team

Smaller sports tend to gravitate to the sports with the bigger teams like swimming, who have critical mass and can make their own party. There are tales of the canoeists and the sailors gravitating towards the rowing team, for example.

4. Same sport, different national team

Apparently British female fencers used to have an affinity with the Hungarian male fencers (who used to win a lot of gold medals). Less so the Russians, who were 'very insular, and it was still the Cold War; it wouldn't have been very patriotic'. The Hungarian/Brit relations highlights one of the asymmetries of the Olympics. Gold medallist men are more successful with women, than gold medallist women are with men. Perhaps the male ego is intimidated by the female success.

The multinational liaisons are much less common than the other three above, partly because of language and partly because of human nature, as a Beijing Olympian from Britain set out.

'You tend to stick to the people you know. I wouldn't say nations mixed that much but I remember hanging out with the Germans quite a bit, guys I knew from the circuit – you might go to a few parties with them. But you tend to stick to your own, you haven't really got enough time [to develop new friendships] unless you're a really sociable person.'

Why waste time getting to know new people, when there are plenty of options already warmed up and ready to take part?

5. Volunteers and marketing professionals

The likes of Speedo, Nike, Adidas and Red Bull employ an army of marketing and promotional professionals, many of whom are 20-something girls who are very easy on the eye. These make a popular alternative. The army of volunteers also provide willing opportunities. An LA athlete put it, 'Oh, yes, there were quite a lot of relations blossoming between athletes. And also with some of the staff, the volunteers. There was quite a lot of that going on. Mainly all short-term relationships. They all came back to reality afterwards.'

6. Different sport, different team

Rarest of all, the unicorn of the Olympic Village, an illicit liaison between athletes of a different sport and from different national teams.

Almost as rare is the sexual encounter that leads to something long term. Just occasionally, with emotions running high and the intensity of the whole experience, bonds can form quickly enough to last. You can find love. Susie Murphy referenced British track and field Olympians from Tokyo, Robbie Brightwell and Ann Packer, who married (the Posh and Becks of the British Olympic team) and then reeled off a host of fencing couples who went onto marriage. The Halsteds, for example. Both teammates of Susie's, Nick Halsted fenced in Mexico, whilst Clare fenced in Munich and Montreal. They met through the sport and the fencing pair produced Laurence Halsted who is now one of Britain's top foil fencers and a likely competitor at London 2012. Hilary Cawthorne overlapped with Susie in Montreal and married Jim Philbin, who represented GB in Los Angeles. Today Hilary Philbin is the Fencing Manager for LOCOG. Singletons looking for love, ignore dating websites. Start fencing.

And it was lucky for Roger Federer that he opted to stay in the Olympic Village in Sydney. It's where he met fellow Swiss tennis player Mirka Vavrinec, whom he married almost 10 years later. Roger Federer, exceptional across so many dimensions; most Olympians can't manage Village liaisons lasting more than ten minutes.

Weightlessness

Athens
21 August 2004

We've moved on, into a smaller nightclub. The party is still on.

    I'm completely absorbed in dancing. Totally unselfconscious. Everyone on the dance floor is on the same kind of Olympic high. It feels simultaneously as if I've been dancing endlessly and for no time at all. I don't feel even slightly tired. I could do this forever. I raise my arms in recognition of a particularly euphoric tune and realise that the stars are twinkling above us.

I get knocked out of my trance and dragged off the dance floor by an attractive Greek girl, who turns out to be a shipping magnate's daughter. Sounds promising. She is only after me for one thing. Sadly it's my GB Team Swatch watch, which I trade with her for two 100m final tickets. When I slip the watch off I realise it's past 5am. Time to go.

I find Jamie sitting at a table to one side in deep and drunken discussions with a German competitor we've raced at several World Champs. A British gold medallist stands to one side like a statue. A girl is pawing him but he looks totally oblivious.

Grabbing Jamie, I stagger outside and end up in a big square. I think this is the Plaka. All around are slumbering bodies or canoodling couples. Already the sun is coming up. It feels oppressively strong to my tired eyes and suddenly I feel the overwhelming urge to get to bed.

I push Jamie into a taxi. Half way home, the driver tries to throw us out as some unhappy gurgling noises erupt from Jamie. I placate the cab driver with a Team GB pin badge. Back in our room I grab another team member and we help Jamie to bed and get him a bin. For a while we amuse ourselves playing 'Jamie buckaroo', posing around his passed out body taking stupid photos. Then the vomiting starts.

Four hours later, Jamie and I are in the back of a minibus getting a lift to watch the racing with some of the women's team who have their Olympic final early this afternoon. The vomiting lasted about an hour and a half but, amazingly, Jamie looks OK. A bit pale maybe. We've been glugging Powerade. The blue one. The girls sitting in front of us are totally silent and focused as we drive to the venue. Medallists at the last Olympics. They have a real shot at gold.

Jamie interrupts my thoughts by grabbing my leg suddenly. An urgent look of complete horror is in his eyes, he has his hand in front of his mouth. He starts to shake with silent retching, like an extra in the movie Aliens. He looks pleadingly at me. I give him a glare as I realise what he's begging me for with his eyes. I unzip my rucksack as quietly and quickly as I can and hand it to him. Impressively silent, he half fills it with blue vomit while I open the back window. I'll swap for his rucksack later.

Two minutes later, we pull up at the competition venue. The girls disembark none the wiser and we wish them solemn good lucks. I head to the competitors' stand to cheer them on. Jamie takes my sloshing rucksack and makes for the physio tent to find a spare massage table to sleep on.

politics and perfect moments

Into the colosseum

Athens
22 August 2004

I share a ride into the Olympic park on a 'civilian' bus with Beth, my long-suffering girlfriend. She hasn't seen much of me for months and the last few days haven't been much better. Tonight we actually get to share an Olympic experience, the 100m final. The fastest man on earth is crowned this evening. Last night I was so smug and overexcited I was made to do several drinking fines by jealous teammates. The tickets are like gold dust. Even some Olympic medallists can't get in.

At the Olympic park we weave our way along with the flow of the crowds and wait in line for security. I'm in team issue casual wear of Union Jack emblazoned polo-shirt and I've given Beth a Team GB cap. In a rare thoughtful moment I managed to do a trade with a diminutive girl on the team who handily has a six-foot boyfriend. Both our better halves are wearing their Team GB shirts tonight. None of the rest of the crowd bats an eyelid. Everyone is decked out in their country's colours. Germans with yellow, red and black Deutschland flags painted on their cheeks. Aussies decked fully in gold and green. Everyone's buzzing with anticipation. It's the politest and happiest queue I've seen.

Once we get to the other side of the fence the crowd disperses. Some peel off to the aquatic centre, some to the hall that hosts the trampolining and gymnastics and others to the velodrome, where different stories will be written tonight. Plenty more head into the various boutiques selling official Olympic merchandise and flags. I almost buy an Athens 2004 dressing gown with matching slippers but Beth manages to talk me down. I already have 35kg of Athens gear she rightly points out.

The luckiest visitors share our walk up to the amphitheatre of the Olympic stadium which is crowned with a huge curved steel arch, a bit like a squeezed version of the new Wembley. Inside, the intimidating superstructure surrounds the field of play, where the athletes will fight for our love and adoration. It feels every bit the colosseum if you can ignore the 50ft-high firelighter roaring with Olympic flame at the far end. The intensity of the lights lining the stadium rim is breathtaking. It's brighter than day in here. All the better for the cameras and the millions watching at home.

Our ticket stubs lead us to seats almost at the very front, four rows from the track and directly behind the 100m start line. Taking in the stadium from our seats, a huge slice is filled with cameras and studios so each national broadcaster can present coverage direct from the Olympic stadium. Why they can't film in studios elsewhere against a blue screen and let another 15,000 people in for the experience of their lives I don't know. But then again the journalists' accreditation is second only to the athletes' accreditation – access almost all areas and I suppose the TV networks are paying hundreds of millions for the rights.

Further round, up behind us, I spot the athletes' box, where post competition medallists can watch others join their club. Gratifyingly, it's rather further away from the action than our seats. I see a couple of my team have made it in. I can't help giving a salute and grinning a little smugly at my location. One of the gold medallists mouths 'What the f**k?' waving his hands in the air good naturedly. Another team member looks rather annoyed that I should have a better view than he does which only serves to make me enjoy it all the more. I heard later on that the same gold medallist upped and left in disgust when one of our surprise medallists entered the box, the latter still in fine spirit having been partying more or less non-stop for the last 48 hours since his shock victory. There are only so many TV talk shows and sponsorship deals up for grabs and there are more than the expected number of British gold medallists. The irritated gold medallist may not have a degree in economics but he sure understands supply and demand.

As a spectator, I hadn't realised how many events take place simultaneously at an athletics event. It's like trying to watch four spinning plates. Watching on TV makes it so much easier; they select your spinning plate for you and switch between them, but it loses the colour of the evening. I also hadn't realised that the 100m semi-finals take place the same night as the finals. Many athletes have days between rounds so they can recover physically but also have time to get their heads right. The idea of getting psyched up for the semi, dealing with the elation of success or the disappointment of a bad run, before bringing yourself down and then almost immediately having to mentally fire up and go out and perform in the final is completely alien to most of us.

Neither of our guys, Mark Lewis-Francis or Jason Gardener, make it through the semi-finals so we decide to adopt the laid back Jamaican Asafa Powell for the final. Difficult to cheer for an American with their self-recognised dominance in track and field.

While the stadium waits for the 100m final, the discus kicks off. Beth comments that the fashion police will be out for Lithuania's Virgilijus Alekna, in his unfetching primary yellow top, bottle green shorts, black trainers and white socks. You wouldn't say it to his face; he looks like a bad guy that should be boxing Stallone in a Rocky movie. The big man spins on the tips of his toes far more nimbly than his truck-like build would suggest possible and throws an Olympic record in his first round throw. The crowd recognises his achievement with a lengthy cheer but he looks remarkably underwhelmed. Difficult to warm to.

In the second round we pick out Robert Fazekas of Hungary with his designer goatee beard, much more appearance-orientated than Alenka. Watching Fazekas I see each thrower has a pre-spin routine, like a golfer before his shot. He bellows like a bull after releasing his disc which soars. Another Olympic record.

Apart from enjoying the name of another Hungarian competitor, Zoltan Kovago, who is also a roarer when he releases his disc, after the excitement of *the first two rounds the next four are a bit of a damp squib. The other competitors are understandably phazed at having already seen two Olympic records. Alenka seems to be trying too hard and only manages one more throw that isn't disqualified for a foot fault or other flaw invisible to us novices. Fazekas is crowned champion, then Alekna and Zoltan.*

As the other competitions gradually conclude, the sprinters come out for the 100m final. What the crowd and the world have been waiting for. The competitors each look remarkably relaxed and warm up with a couple of practice starts in their lanes. A couple change their tops into final race gear and reveal their muscular perfection. It's like they've been hewn from stone. I feel fat. When did I last work out?

Defending champion, Maurice Greene exudes an earth-moving self-confidence. His younger compatriot Justin Gatlin is easier to like, having only turned pro two years ago. We're still rooting for Jamaica. As the sprinters take their marks complete silence falls across the thousands in the stadium and no doubt millions of households watching on TV.

In the next 30 seconds the fastest man on earth will be crowned. The world is watching. What will the champion say to the world?

Perfect moments?

Just two days after our trip to the stadium, discus champion Robert Fazekas was expelled from Athens and the grumpy Lithuanian Alekna was promoted to the gold. Fazekas only squeezed a few drops of urine (25mg) in his post-competition dope test, the minimum being 75mg. An IOC source said he'd also been caught trying to switch his urine sample. Fazekas was the 16th athlete to be expelled from the Athens Olympics. Whilst one Olympic record was stripped from him, he simultaneously helped set another.

Fazekas wasn't to be the only deposed Hungarian gold medallist of Athens. The wonderfully named Adrian Annus arrived in Athens as one of the favourites for the hammer. He delivered and won gold, passed his post-competition drug test, unlike countryman Fazekas, and almost immediately drove home to Hungary. No partying for Mr Annus. A few days later the head of Athens doping control revealed that Annus's pre-competition test of the 18 August and his urine sample given on the night of his victory probably belonged to different people. Annus refused to appear for another test and was disqualified. It was never officially concluded how Annus provided samples from two different people, but there were rumours of a fake bladder device which held the 'clean' urine and which could be emptied in the test pot when required.

In the 100m, Justin Gatlin beat the favourites and was crowned champion. Beth managed to get down the front row and shake Justin's hand, saying, 'Well done, Maurice'. I doubt it burst his bubble. Gatlin went on to a bronze medal in the USA 1–2–3 in the 200m and a silver in the 4 x 100m relay behind a stunning gold for our boys. A few years later, rather than a few days, Gatlin was himself at the centre of a doping storm, failing a test for testosterone in 2006 and receiving a four-year ban.

I'd applauded wildly at Robert Fazekas's record-breaking discus throw. I'd whooped at the 100m. Do the subsequent doping issues make me a fool for cheering and make us all fools for watching? I don't think so. Each Olympics makes great stories, good and bad, and every story needs both heroes and villains. One of the classic Olympic moments which happens every four years is the contrast between the pin-drop silence before a 100m final and the eruption of 20,000 camera flashes and ten seconds of manic cheering. Other Olympic moments are more unique. Native Australian Kathy Freeman winning the 400m in Sydney; Steven Redgrave rowing to his fifth consecutive gold in Sydney; Michael Phelps swimming to his eighth medal in Athens; Eric the Eel, from Equatorial Guinea, setting a new personal best in the 100m freestyle in Sydney, notwithstanding that it was still more than double the time of his slowest competitors; British 400m runner Derek Redmond tearing his hamstring in the semi-final in Barcelona and being helped round the remainder of the lap by his dad, to a standing ovation; Usain Bolt's 100m in Beijing.

The Olympics delivers these moments of hope and greatness which unite countries and, occasionally, unite the world. I was lucky enough to be in the stadium the night Kelly Holmes started imprinting herself into the British public consciousness, winning her first gold medal of the Games in the 800m, having sat almost last at half way (like a good Brit I was preparing myself for disappointment at that point). I still remember the buzz and the moment, and the members of the crowd from other nations turning to congratulate us as if we had won the gold ourselves. In the crowd there was an astonishing feeling of togetherness across all nations, the like of which I've only experienced at Olympic competitions.

Once their competitions are over, the Olympians hungrily lap up the opportunity to watch other sports. Elite athletes tend to be obsessed not just about their sports but others too. They know what it takes to make it and get dementedly interested in the rules and tactics of sports new to them. Here's an Athens and Beijing Olympian from Team GB.

'You can party anytime, anywhere. But the Olympics are a unique opportunity to go and see other sports and how other top athletes perform. And those experiences in Athens really benefited me when it came to competing in Beijing. And I made a deliberate attempt to make the most out of both Olympics sports wise. The partying was fun, but really it's important to get a broader sense of what Olympic sport is about. I tried to see sports I wouldn't see on TV. Water polo, wrestling, kayaking, hockey. It all reminds you that a lot of success is about seizing opportunities.'

A first-time Olympian in Sydney was a little more jaded but still made the effort.

'I went to see loads in Sydney but I can't remember a lot of it because I'd had an hour's sleep and then went out again. Apart from the evening stuff, by the time you went to track and field, which was kind of the standard evening thing before going out again, by that stage you'd started to recover enough that you could begin to enjoy life again.'

I asked a triple Olympian whether as an athlete she could just walk into whatever she fancied (I kind of knew the answer, having missed out on cycling and having had to make do with the Greco-Roman wrestling in Athens, but I wanted to check it was the same at other Games).

'It would be great if you could just stroll in but each Olympic team is given a certain number of tickets. You put in your application at the Village each evening and then later, there's a ballot. So you come in from your night out as the sun comes up and go straight to the Team HQ and find out what tickets you've got for the day. That's certainly what happens with the bigger teams. With the smaller teams it's easier; our Irish mates got plenty. Beijing was really bad because they didn't actually give out that many tickets so it got to the point where we would just turn up to events anyway and just say, "Look there's no one in the athletes' stands." It seemed such a shame that there was hardly anybody in the athletes' stands. That's part of being at the Olympics isn't it, to go and watch all these different events?'

Outside the official Olympian channels, the black market is open to athletes like everyone else but pricing often precludes them. In Beijing, Michael Phelps' success and resultant skyrocketing demand from American supporters saw tickets to the Water Cube hit more than $1,000 a throw. It was the same story with British supporters and tickets for the Velodrome. In Sydney, a sizeable part of the Australian team got round the issue on the night of Cathy Freeman's final by storming security and telling them to take it up with the Prime Minister.

However athletes experience the Games, many Olympians talk about the feeling of unity with other nations; a oneness with those of other countries and religions. Here's another triple Olympian.

'I feel very privileged to have experienced the feeling of unity with other nations the Olympics gives you. It overcomes all the political shit that's going on in the world. Actually, the basis is we all get on, ordinary people get on. It's just other interventions that get in the way. Even if you couldn't speak each other's language you had this feeling of unity. You were sportsmen in common. Whatever sport it was, you knew they'd worked as hard as you to get where you were. It was amazing.'

Steve Batchelor agreed, 'That's the beauty of the Olympics. A lot of the time there will be countries at war competing at the same Games and you're in there as athletes and there is not a problem. Not a problem. It's like, why are they fighting each other? They're just like us. It brings people together.'

Despite the controversies and the doping, the unity and the perfect moments remain in the consciousness. The Games is still worth having. Jacques Rogge noted in his closing address in Athens, 'You have 10,500 athletes in the Olympic Village, you do not have 10,500 saints. You will always have cheats.'

He's right, cheating is not new. Even at the Ancient Greek Olympics, where it is easy to assume the naked athletes competing under the hot sun did so purely for honour and glory, human nature intervened. Back in 388 BC Eupolos from Thessaly bribed his boxing opponents to let him win, so he could be champion. They were all fined.

Athletes 'nationality hopping' to increase their chances of Olympic selection isn't new either. At the 69th Olympic festival in Ancient Greece, Sotades, a Cretan, won the long-distance running race. By the next festival he was competing as an Ephesian, having been bribed by the Ephesians. He was banished by the Cretans.

Even the athletes showboating to boost their marketing endorsement dollars and to flame their fame is ancient news. Milo of Croton was five-time consecutive wrestling champion from the 62nd to 66th Olympiad, 532 to 516 BC. One of the most legendary athletes in the ancient world, Milo, rather a showman, wore a lion skin cloak and used to show off by tying cords round his forehead, holding his breath and snapping them with his bulging forehead veins. To satisfy his Olympic appetite for meat, he once carried into the stadium a four-year old bull across his shoulders which he promptly slaughtered and ate. Milo makes Usain Bolt look shy and demure.

The conflict between the high ideals of the Olympic spirit and the crude pressures of commercialism and rivalry to succeed have always been present. Whilst the worldwide TV and media coverage of the Games pipes the regular controversies into living rooms globally, the Games can also be used as a platform to point to even greater human evils. Governments clumsily wield Olympic boycotts, to the detriment of their athletes, to make political statements, but it is the conduct of individual competitors that we remember. The four gold medals of black athlete Jesse Owens at Hitler's 1936 Games, elegantly flawing Hitler's Aryan ideals, is often noted. Susie Murphy fenced in Mexico 32 years later. 'I was in the stadium when Tommie Smith put on the black glove symbolising Black Power. You try to keep politics out of sport but it rears its head every now and again. The Olympics is a huge platform for people making statements.'

Tommie Smith and John Carlos, who took gold and bronze in the 200m in 1968, raised black gloved hands in silent protest at racial discrimination during the American national anthem, and received their medals shoeless to represent black poverty. They were expelled from the Games but the point had been well made.

Susie was regularly fencing against Soviet Union competitors, just a few years after the Cuban Missile Crisis, with East and West still threatening nuclear apocalypse on each other. Were they at each other's throats?

'After first fighting [Olympic Champion] Novikova in Mexico I fought her in other competitions, the World Championships and other Olympics. You could tell she had a tremendous respect for us. She was a wonderful fencer and a very nice lady. Even though we didn't speak each other's language there was a respect there and we got on well.'

Soon after the Mexico Games, Romanian champion fencer Ion Drimba defected across to the West, highlighting the plight of people under Communism. It became a double blow for the USSR as Drimba started to coach in the USA where he was a significant driver in their emergence in international fencing.

It was four years after Mexico, in Munich, when the most famous of political interventions at an Olympics took place. Susie Murphy was there as the terrorists struck.

'That part of it was just surreal. I was in the Village and remember going down in the morning to catch the bus to go training. Under the Village it was like Victoria bus station, buses taking all the sports off to their venues. The German police stopped me. "You're not going anywhere; go back to your room." That was when the PLO had fired on the Israeli athletes, one of whom was a fencer. I remember being in the Village and seeing them [PLO terrorists] on the balcony with the black masks on. Then the helicopters came in and picked them up. We all had to stay back and then the Olympics carried on afterwards. It was bizarre. It all went pear shaped. They all got killed.'

Bittersweet endings

The Olympics can produce rare horrors which only serve to remind us of the importance of international unity. Most Olympics don't end as poignantly as Munich (with athletes of all nations and religions, singing along to 'Give Peace a Chance' in the Olympic Village disco) but the closing ceremonies are always bittersweet. For the Olympic city and its people, the moment in the international spotlight is almost over. For the volunteers and the spectators, tomorrow it's back to the day job. A fraction of the competitors waving from the centre of the stadium have a gold medal round their necks, a far greater number are torturing themselves about their performance or are stung by self-doubt. Regardless of their result almost all are hurting from sleep deprivation and cumulative colossal hangovers, but at least they're not paranoid about how the next few hours will affect their performance. Closing ceremonies remain no less spectacular than their Opening Ceremony brethren though, and walking into the arena is just as breathtaking, as double Olympian Bas van de Goor agreed: 'You never forget the time you enter the stadium and realise you are at the exact centre of the world at that moment.'

Here's a triple British Olympian on her memories of her closing ceremonies (notably she'd only been to one opening ceremony across her three Olympics – if you want to spot athletes and you're only going to watch one of the ceremonies, make it the closing ceremony).

'Marching in, it is even more disorderly. There's no kind of lining up in height order it's just like "Go at it, guys". You march in, and I was lucky enough to be part of pretty successful teams. We're all wearing our medals and I remember being very proud of what we all achieved and simultaneously sad that it's all coming to an end. So it's really kind of weird. It's like being back at the start where you're trying to take everything in and remember every moment of it but you know there's only minutes left of it, that it's coming to an end.'

The Olympians march round the track and take position in the centre in their allocated team slot, not that it stays that way for long.

'Everyone's just super excited. You can't keep a lid on it. You don't have to be sensible anymore. However much they try to keep you in a certain place for the worldwide pictures, they kind of try to pen you in, everyone just runs around and catches up with people, causing mischief and mayhem. In the centre you can't really hear the music either, so you've actually got no idea what's going on, so you're just entertaining yourselves. It's so much fun. In Beijing they also had the big screen, like a banner round the edge of the stadium playing all sorts of different Olympic moments on a loop. They showed our race.

'In Sydney I remember being at the closing ceremony and they had these big inflatables. When they released them we started using them as trampolines. We managed to get the Thorpedo on one and we were tossing him up in the air. He had massive feet. I think I've got some pictures. He was petrified.'

The melange of athletes in the middle allows for some last minute flirting. A Beijing silver medallist remembered. 'I do remember giving my flat cap to a major Dutch swimmer because she was being ridiculously flirtatious with me on the march out of the stadium and talking about how much she enjoyed the cap.' The Olympian refused to divulge whether there were other exchanges later on.

A British gold medallist from Beijing chips in with his memories of the closing moments of the ceremony.

'They had this tower of people doing all these amazing things and at the bottom was this little one volunteer who seemed to have a throng of people around him. This volunteer came into the crowds of athletes [in the middle of the stadium] and wormed his way right past us. It turned out it was Jackie Chan surrounded by bodyguards. It was awesome. Really random. Then we had the 'British eight minutes' leading onto the next Olympics. That red bus that came on. God that was embarrassing. Although I was 10m from Jimmy Page playing 'Whole Lot of Love'. That was one of the highlights of the whole Olympic experience, even though Leona Lewis was singing.'

In the final moments, after the speeches, the focus turns to the Olympic flame. The triple Olympian picks up the thread once more.

'Everybody, regardless of how much messing around is going on in the middle, with catching up and flag waving and stuff, when the ceremony turns to the torch, everyone kind of just simmers down. Then when it goes out there is definitely a kind of special moment.'

The flame goes out and suddenly four years of your life is abruptly over. The next chapter is opened but the pages are blank. Terrifying.

'You kind of think, "Oh my God, that's it they just turned out the light". And then the fireworks go off and it's cool – the world's not finished. And then everyone carries on.'

After the closing ceremony ends, the after party begins. Tom James remembers events in Beijing:

'We were all invited back to a party in the Olympic Village. The Team GB management had somehow managed to sneak in 4,000 bottles of beer into their offices. We had a big barbeque, had some music playing, everyone was mingling. No other country had organised a party in the Olympic Village. There were a couple of Aussies sitting outside their lodge trying to have some good fun but everyone started turning up at our party. No other country had bothered to do that. It was awesome. Pete Reed administered a human pyramid. I think we got seven layers up. On the bottom we had some rowers, judo guys and boxers, on another layer we had some hockey guys and then smaller and smaller until at the top we had Beth Tweddle the gymnast. She scooted up and did a little somersault off the top. Nowhere else would you find such perfect specimens for the different ranks of the human pyramid. No one cared about getting injured or falling over. The Games are over, it's party time.'

Having arrived as one team, on the return flight home the athletes, in Team GB at least, find themselves segmented, gold medallists into First Class, then as many medallists as can be fitted into Business Class, before the rest return in the back of the plane. Not that it makes much difference to the athletes. Here's a silver medallist.

'I remember boarding the flight home from Beijing and the steward coming up to pour champagne.'

No doubt the steward excitedly wanted to help celebrate Team GB's fantastic Olympic performance and bag an autograph or two.

'He was so disappointed. No one in the whole cabin wanted champagne because we were all so broken. I'd been up the whole night before. I passed out before we even took off and woke up on the tarmac at Heathrow. Beijing to London flat out. I didn't even stir.'

reborn

Aftershocks

London
18 October 2004

Busy day. First the celebratory bus parade around London, which ended with a jamboree in Trafalgar Square. Now we're inside Buckingham Palace about to meet the Queen. Later on, the British Olympic Association is putting on an after party at Hamleys, the enormous toy store on Regent Street. Jamie reckons it'll be better than the one on the London Eye after Sydney.

Looking down over the crowds in Trafalgar Square I couldn't restrain a wave. They had no idea who I was but they waved back, surprisingly adoringly, with little Union Jacks fluttering. Could definitely get used to it.

We've all come back from the Games different people. Some of us have been reborn national heroes. Some, like me, have started new careers, others are just revelling or drowning sorrows. I'm already getting bored of the reflex question after people discover you've been to the Olympics.

'Did you get a medal?'

Our return has brought division in the team. Only a few get the invites on to GMTV. Even fewer get passed the microphone. Popular consciousness only has room for a handful of Olympian household names. As one of the lads said on the bus tour, 'There's only room for one gold medallist on the cereal box'.

Half an hour ago the medal ceremony in the throne room concluded. It was just like the end of Star Wars *after the rebels have destroyed the Death Star. Just swap Princes Leia for Princess Anne handing out the medals, add Prince Philip standing to one side and the Queen on her throne and then trade the rebels for the whole of Team GB lined up in ranks and Go For Gold pinstripe suits.*

Equestrian Leslie Law replaced Luke Skywalker (making small talk easy for Princess Anne), receiving his gold medal for individual eventing after his German competitor went through the start line twice and lost at the Court of Arbitration for Sport. It was a triple bonus for Team GB, as fellow individual eventer Pippa Funnell got upgraded to bronze and the German team were stripped of their team gold, upgrading our whole eventing team to silver. Plenty of happy horse-people for Princess Anne to talk to. Chris Newton and Bryan Steel, members of the cycling pursuit team, looked even happier getting their silver medals having originally been denied them after taking part in the heats and not the final.

Now we're in a long gallery, through from the throne room. Silver salvers filled with champagne and delicious treats are whisked between us. It's wonderful to eat and drink without fear about tomorrow.

We've had the briefing. Talk amongst yourselves in small groups of half a dozen or so. Let her address you first. Mam as in jam, not Marm as in arm. Our team manager has lined us up in a crescent. Are those tiny beads of sweat on his brow?

A gaggle of other Olympians, I think sailors, open their formation suddenly to reveal the Queen, who walks up to us. Wow, she is absolutely tiny. The team manager walks her along our crescent introducing us and now profusely sweating. Rather suddenly it's my turn.

'Mam, may I introduce ...' the team manager starts but I lose track of his voice. The Queen is staring disappointedly at my clip on bow tie. I suddenly feel completely naked.

'Aeint what did you dooo?' she asks politely, not looking that interested.

I answer, but again she doesn't look that interested and her expression doesn't change. I can't blame her. There are far more interesting athletes here. Now we're back, not all Olympians are equal.

Welcome home

Depending on which Olympian you speak to, the homecoming is either the best bit or the moment you realise you're not a superhuman. Sometimes there are crowds waiting for you at the airport, in most cases not. Either way, it's wonderful to wrap your arms around your parents and loved ones having been away for months on an emotional roller-coaster and returned to an uncertain future. An Athens medallist fondly remembered landing at Gatwick.

'When you walk off the plane you're in this three tier world. You're a non-medallist, a non-gold medallist or a gold medallist. They kept all the medallists back, took our bags round to a press conference area and we just kind of walked out and there were huge crowds and heaps of people down to see us. I remember my Dad being there and giving me a flag as we walked through. It was close to my sister's school so loads of her kids came down and stuff. It was huge. Because you've been cocooned from it all so you don't realise how much excitement there is at home. And you walk out and you think, "Wow, all these people have actually been watching and it means so much to them". It's such a great feeling to think that you've influenced some small part of the country and made them excited about something.'

Unfortunately after Beijing, perhaps with the over-performance of the team, the return was over-sanitised and lost the magic, as the same Olympian recalls.

'After Beijing it was really sad. They thought that so many people were going to turn up so they then didn't let us go through the right way. They made us go into the Princess's special suite or whatever when we landed and we were bussed to a hotel where they had a reception for the media. But it wasn't the same, you didn't get Joe Public, you didn't get the people who had been watching, you got the media who claimed they watched. You were just back in this media circus where people might or might not want to interview you. By this time you want to see your friends and family. You don't need any more of that. You want people to be excited for you, you don't want to be in a press conference.'

Steve Batchelor remembers the return of his gold medal hockey team after Seoul with mixed emotion.

'For the last few days of the Olympics I was waiting for the plane, I just wanted to go home and to my wife-to-be. We were put in first class on this jumbo, the whole of the hockey squad, which was quite nice. We came back into Heathrow and the police surrounded us and took our bags and put them in a pile. We had no idea what was happening in England about us at the time. Absolutely no idea that it had gone absolutely nuts here. I still get people coming up to me saying. "I watched your final". So, when we came out of the airport there were thousands of people. It was just bizarre, absolutely bizarre. And we went straight onto breakfast TV. Back home the whole village and the school came up to my parents' house and there were big banners and that.'

Having become the ultimate hockey team of 1988 (with three minutes to go in the final, the coach brought on the substitutes who hadn't had a chance to play in the tournament, to ensure that they too got gold medals), on their return cracks began to occur.

'I'm hopeless at scoring goals and I'm a forward. I set Sean [Curley] up with loads. It didn't bother me scoring. I much preferred setting up a good goal. That and when I shot I always seemed to miss. I got quite jealous of Sean because he got all the attention, the coverage and appearances. I got quite jealous of the whole thing. Sean Curley is the famous hockey player. Everyone always asks me whether I know Sean. We used to live near each other and were really close mates. We both received keys to our town and all that sort of stuff which was quite amusing. But everybody wanted to see him and speak to him. So I found that quite difficult.'

Even later, showing me a video of the '88 final, Steve comments as he's skillfully dribbling the ball in the opposition's D before laying it off with laser precision to a teammate, 'Curley would have shot from there.'

After Olympians settle in back home and recover from the initial welcome home parties, the invitations start dropping onto the doormat. The more successful meet with agents and get deals struck, but all of us get the two big invitations, in my case now proudly framed in my parents' downstairs toilet.

Firstly, a thick, gold edged and embossed invitation from the Queen, shortly followed by one from the Prime Minister, in my case, Tony and Mrs Blair, to an event at Lord's cricket ground to celebrate the Athens Olympic team's achievements and to support the London 2012 bid (we'll all have to keep our wits about us around Cherie, thought I).

Olympic gold medallist Tom James fondly remembers the official celebrations around London after Beijing.

'I remember when we got back, doing the bus rides: that was awesome. So many people were out cheering and you just wave back, gobsmacked. We stopped in Trafalgar Square and there were 30,000 people there or something. We were presented to the crowd after the cyclists. Because I was bow of the four I was going to lead the group out. I came out and stuck my arms up and whooped and the whole crowd went apeshit. It was absolutely awesome. I remember waving for ages and people taking pictures and everyone cheering. Then I got dragged back [to go out with the rest] and there were some jokey boos because I was leaving the stage. I just remember that moment so well. It was just awesome.'

While a parade in London just about cuts the mustard for Britain, as a medallists-only celebration in Paris does for France and an Olympic team procession through the canals of Amsterdam does in Holland, countries with bigger landmasses and more dispersed populations, like the US and Australia, have to spread the Olympic feel-good factor with a concerted programme of events.

An American gold medallist remembers his tour of the country with other Olympians after Los Angeles. Being America, naturally it was commercially-funded, this time by 7-Eleven.

'They took us round the country on a chartered plane. It was kind of fun and mainly an excuse to drink inordinate amounts of alcohol. There was a ticker tape parade down Fifth Avenue, New York City. We stayed in the Plaza Hotel, a real famous hotel, and that night we were VIPs at the Limelight nightclub. In its day the Limelight was a big deal, like Studio 54 today, there was a queue a mile long. It's in a converted church. It was exclusive and exotic, women dancing in go-go cages. Mostly I remember the music being incredibly loud and it being very smokey. And we also got to meet the President, not in the Limelight I should clarify.'

The Australians put on a similar national tour. Here's a double Aussie Olympian:

'They do a ticker tape parade round the country. If you don't medal [like me in Barcelona] you're on the back of a Ute. You literally jumped on the back and there might be a token three people who shake your hand in each town. And you drive across the seven states. Post Atlanta '96 it was bigger and I was a medallist. Medallists got flown round state to state to state and I have to say I had to be helped off the plane on some occasions. It was sensational. In each state you get receptions and functions and get paraded round in the back of cars wearing your medals. I had a year off after Atlanta and the buzz didn't go away that whole year, a lot of it was to warm up for Sydney. After Sydney weirdly the buzz just stopped immediately.

'I think the events back home probably had more impact on me than when I was at the Games. I was invited to the Melbourne Cup and I remember being able to go from corporate tent to corporate tent to corporate tent. It only ever happened once. I could get into anywhere. I even met Prince Philip, Germaine Greer and my future husband on the same day.'

'My favourite was after Barcelona. I'd missed out on my friend's black tie 21st birthday but I did get to party on the top of Mount Kosciuszko with all the other federal athletes. We all got absolutely wasted on the pinnacle of Australia. It happened to be snowing in the middle of summer up there and some of us got snow blindness. Even better, I got it all fully funded from the Australian Institute of Sport's recreational budget. You might have to make sacrifices but you also get opportunities.'

Most British athletes point to the visit to Buckingham Palace and meeting royalty as their post-Games highlight. Susie Murphy went to three Olympics but only got to meet the Queen once.

'After Mexico we weren't invited back. Two athletes sat on the throne in the Throne Room and I don't think the Queen took too kindly to that. We'd blotted our copy book.'

Thankfully, after a decade or so Her Majesty forgave the errant Olympians and re-started the tradition of British teams visiting the Palace after the Olympics. It's still not always a smooth ride when she meets the team. After Beijing, one Olympian from the armed forces who'd been through Sandhurst with Prince William and Harry took immense pleasure in telling the Queen she had, 'two very naughty grandsons'. The Queen apparently nodded knowingly.

Over-excited Olympians can get over-familiar with other members of royalty too. One Beijing Olympian confides.

'Yeah, we met Princess Anne quite a few times, at the Ambassadors' reception before and at the Palace after. Then we met her at one of the Olympic Gold balls. One of my teammates, typical for him, just went straight in and grabbed her by the shoulders and kissed her on the cheek. She stood back looking a bit shocked and said, "I didn't realise we knew each other that well." You forget they're royalty. You're not meant to go up and just kiss them on the cheek, you know. Daughter of the Queen and all that.'

After Athens, Tom James also made an impact at the Palace for the wrong reasons when he met the Queen.

'The first time I met her was quite awkward. Because we didn't win a gold medal we weren't part of the group that saw her in the first chamber. So we were in the long gallery with the "common" Olympians which was quite crowded. Everyone was having drinks. I'd had a few whiskies and needed the toilet. I saw an opening in the crowd and went for it. Suddenly I was in the middle of this circle of people on my own. I tried to squeeze through to escape and brushed against someone who had their back to me who was talking to someone else. The Queen turned around and I almost jumped and gave an embarrassingly huge intake of breath. Thankfully David Tanner [the rowing team manager] was there to introduce me to her and she was really nice. I had no idea what to say. I was like, "Yes, yes, yes." She was really sweet, saying "Don't be nervous, don't be shy, don't be shy." She sort of speaks to you half listening with glazed eyes and drifts over to the next person. They never really engage with you because they've got to see so many people. But it was pretty special. Then I went to the toilet and felt like a right idiot.'

Thankfully, Tom got to put it right after his gold in Beijing.

'The next time around [with a gold medal] was really nice because we went into a separate room somewhere. We sat in groups of four or five people and the Queen would come and chat to each group for a good five or six minutes. I remember sitting there with Rebecca Adlington and a few others. And Prince Philip came round. They were really nice and chatty. Then of course the next time was getting the MBE and meeting Prince Charles.'

Royalty is one thing; politicians are another. The athletes don't tend to point to meeting Prime Ministers as highlights. It feels rather too much like a staged PR opportunity for the politicians.

Here's a Beijing Olympian's reading of Gordon Brown:

'I met him twice, the first time out in Beijing with lots of people around in the Village. It was like he had a few questions prepared and when you responded he'd be lost. It was quite an obviously awkward conversation. You'd say something and he'd be like, "Right, right, right, right, right" not taking anything of it in and already moving onto the next person. Job done. Then you suddenly straightaway meet his wife Sarah Brown, who is completely amiable and really chatty and really talkative. The contrast is amazing. You suddenly realise the stark difference. The awkwardness personified in the press is real. Gordon just couldn't seem able to relax [in public]. When we met him a second time at an Olympic reception in St James's I remember briefly chatting to him. He was much more relaxed and seemed like a nice amiable chap. When he was in front of the lights he had this awkward sort of persona.'

Whatever your view of politicians, the first month or two after a Games is brilliant fun, but it soon bubbles back down. As one Olympian recounts, 'People ask how long were you famous for. I say about two weeks. People briefly recognised us.'

But the recognition thing isn't always easy, as another gold medallist confesses. 'You get a few looks, a few people doing a double check. But it's difficult to know if people recognise you or if you're just having a bad hair day. And you start to look at people thinking they might recognise you but then you looking at them causes them to look back at you and wonder, why is that tall guy staring at me?

As things settle down the Olympians discover who they've become. Gold medallists are forever rebranded Olympic champions. Most others gradually realise that they are still just themselves, but with a few new cocktail party anecdotes. Here's one gold medallist reflecting on his new persona:

'Now that I've got gold medal people definitely treat you differently. People call you a celebrity, whatever celebrity is. I guess I'm on the Z list. It's one of those things. I don't think I fully appreciate the label of the gold medal. It's not something you ever take in properly. When you look at the level of achievement, the people you beat, the people who wanted to get a gold medal but didn't. The chances of getting one are tiny. We brought back 31 individual gold medals from Beijing. There are only about 300 living gold medallists in Great Britain. Out of a population of 60 million. Put it in perspective like that, you're bloody lucky. And a lot of it is luck. It really is.'

the dark side of the moon

Going cold turkey

London
16 November 2004
The Olympics was just months ago but it feels like a different life, one I imag-ined. Now I'm all at sea.

I can't get used to weekends. I feel a desperate but nebulous need to achieve something but mostly Saturday and Sunday are brunches and shopping. Is this it? My girlfriend bought us golf lessons. Something to learn together and to fill the void where sport used to be. For a while I obsessed over golf – on driving ranges, on Google, in books – trying to get good as quickly as possible – but after playing a few rounds the burn melted away. What was the point? I wasn't very good. I was never going to win the Ryder Cup.

My parents clearly miss me being an athlete too. Dad keeps dropping hints about the next Olympics and how wonderful it will be. Mum has just finished sewing me a blanket from some of my old GB kit and international swaps. I now sleep under a patchwork of victories and losses from another life. I guess my sport gave them an excuse to cheer me on and provided a very tangible reason to be proud of me. It's not so easy to talk proudly to relatives about how well your kids are doing when they are only at the early stages of an obscure job in the city. It's only with hindsight I realise my competitions were a good excuse for us to spend lots of time together and share emotional journeys. Only now do I realise they attended every race I ever competed in.

Amazing how quickly I've got used to not setting an alarm on a Friday night. But it's good to lie in, helps to sleep off the hangovers which I'm experiencing a lot more regularly now. For the last decade, whether it was out at parties, socials or even just the pub quiz, in the back of my mind I was thinking about the next race or the next physiological test or just the alarm clock at 7am tomorrow and the three training sessions to get through before being back on the sofa. Getting through one session with a hangover is hard but doable. You can zombie through a couple of hours and cling on till you can get back to bed. Two sessions? Much harder and often a dead giveaway to the coaches when between sessions you're dozing in the corner while the others lunch and stretch. A hangover and three training sessions? You only do that once.

So without three training sessions the next morning I'm having to learn self-control at parties, when most others learnt it when they were 15. Or rather I will have to. Right now I just want to let loose and be the last person to go home, rather than the first. It's not hard – it feels easy – I lack the switch that regulates most people, I still just don't get tired. I can dance and drink and jump up and down for hours and still want more, doing my best to catch up on all the nights out I missed and make up for all the friendships that fell by the wayside because I never had time for people.

The working week is taking a lot of getting used to, both physically and mentally. Now I'm sitting behind a desk for nine or ten hours a day when I'm used to being outside in the sunshine or in the rain. Whether it was hail or snow or sunburn or icy wind, you felt alive. Sometimes when it's raining I pop out of the office and lift my face to the rain, just for the hell of it. Just to feel something.

After an hour or two of work each morning my legs start jiggling uncontrollably under the desk. Sometimes I get that under control only for my feet to start tapping. I crave the endorphins of exercise and go the gym at strange hours to get my hit. I need it, crave it. I've entered the marathon to silence my legs.

I used to get my buzz, my shots of adrenaline, from competing every day, even if it was just a training session at reasonably low intensity. And occasionally, just occasionally, there'd be a hit of another sort – when having a perfect moment on training camp – when my sport just felt natural. Now my treat is leaving the desk for 10 minutes for a Starbucks mocha. And sometimes a cookie.

But I've got to watch the cookies. I met up with some of the old squad on the weekend, where we all put a brave face on and talked about how great it was to be free of training and how we were really enjoying moving on. A couple of the guys are really piling on the weight – you wouldn't believe they represented Great Britain in the Olympics at a tough physical sport earlier this year. Jamie has gone from 90kg to 128kg. All flab. I guess that's what happens when you eat 6,000 calories a day but don't exercise from morning till night. He looks like a fat bloke from the pub wearing a puffa jacket under his T-shirt, not a guy who was recently one of the human race's fittest physical specimens. From Adonis to James Corden. Thank God my previously enormous appetite has receded a little.

I hadn't realised quite how vain I'd become and how proud of the body I'd chiselled over the years. I sometimes find myself flexing in the bathroom mirror to check I've still got arms. Lines of sinew and defined edges of muscle are smoothing away, day by day. The hint of a six pack I'd worked a decade to earn has gone in three months. Even if I went to the gym every night I'd never keep my Olympic physique; almost better never to have had it. And to cap it all, now that I'm an indoor animal my permanent, healthy looking tan is being replaced by an indoorsy pallor.

But the physical shock is the easier half to adjust to. The mental shock is worse. I'd spent years training and competing and got to the top of my sport. I knew everything there was to know about it. No boss and no limits but my own. I was good at something, really good. That little badge on my right breast – the Olympic rings and British flag – it was evidential proof I was different. I wasn't normal. I was special. Now I'm another guy in a suit on the Tube. I suppose some of the other ex-athletes have it worse. They're worse than ordinary, they're unemployed.

Having been at a pinnacle of competence I've crashed down to the bottom rung. I know nothing of any use! I have to ask how to do almost everything. My first appraisal was last week, after three months here (apparently I'm

OK – not good, not awful). I had no idea what they were going to say. Here I feel in limbo. It's not easy to measure performance. There isn't a monitor giving you your average speed or recognition of a personal best. In training I had day-to-day and week-by-week goals, whether in the gym lifting weights or against the stopwatch. Individually they weren't huge but they added up and I could measure and see gradual success – spurring me to the next small victory. I miss the simplicity of sport. Business is much less clear; it seems to be all office politics I can't navigate and goals I'm not interested in. Our company's corporate target, getting £2 billion revenues over the next two years, is difficult to get enthused about when you're at the base of the pyramid.

Waiting three months for my first review felt strange. I'm used to instant, frank feedback from coaches while training and then more analysis and feedback after the session. My coach didn't wait three months to tell me what I was doing wrong or right. Surely it's like training a dog – throw the stick, dog retrieves, give dog treat – dog learns. Dog chews up prized Jimmy Choo shoes, dog gets shouted at and. Dog learns. Wait three months after he's brought your slippers or left a surprise on the carpet before praising or punishing him and you get one confused and stressed dog. Why are we trained any different?

Without the annual rhythm of selection, competition and World Championships and no ultimate, over-arching Olympic target, life and work just kind of roll on and on. The days pass slowly; the months fly by without the milestones of seasonal competition to separate them.

Most of all I miss hanging out with my squad, my really close friends, for most of each day. There was no hierarchy really and we all took responsibility for our own performance. Here I'm on the bottom rung of seven tiers. In the squad we were all working towards a common shared goal, which we gave everything for – relationships, other friends, our lives. At work some guys are already talking to head-hunters looking to desert the team for a slightly bigger pay cheque.

Last night, sensing I was down, Beth put on The Incredibles, *a cheery Disney animated comedy. It depressed me immensely. I was embarrassed to admit I felt a bit like Mr Incredible, in his little office cubicle doing a pointless job. Mr Incredible has hung up his superhero outfit and spends his days reminiscing about the good times with old compatriots and filling his study with photos and cuttings of past glories. He yearns to feel the adrenaline of the chase. The thrill of being different.*

How do you adjust to being, well, normal?

Will I ever feel special again?

Sink or swim

Three months after the closing ceremony the post-Olympic buzz has petered out. The invites stop hitting the doormat. Friends and family have all visited and congratulated or commiserated. Having been totally blinkered and focused solely on the Olympics for years, suddenly the hoods are pulled from their heads and Olympians are left blinking in the sunlight of real life.

Like film stars who make the perfect film aged 22, or astronauts who've walked on the face of the moon in their 30s, Olympians are left asking themselves – what do I with the rest of my life having already achieved everything I wanted?

What the hell do I do now?

Many athletes don't wonder for long. They get back into their sport. Back on the treadmill. Stick to what you know. They have a few months off and then give themselves entirely to the next Olympics. The Commonwealth Games are only two years away after all. Many have real motivation for staying in sport – a belief they can medal if they give it four more years or they feel the need to make amends for a poor performance and put ghosts to rest. But many find themselves back in professional sport without the motivation to be there, either from a lack of other options or a forgivable lack of willingness to move away from their field of expertise. Inevitably these old war horses struggle to find their form and eventually lose out to younger idealists who are truly hungry to make the Games. Better to quit the sport on a high and retain your self respect, than to have it gradually eroded from you until the sport drops you.

Some athletes are persuaded to try other sports by Team GB coaches, particularly since Rebecca Romero picked up a silver rowing in Athens and went one better in Beijing with a gold cycling in the individual pursuit. One of my more explosive friends was head-hunted by the bobsleigh team after Athens. I got a letter from UK Sport saying I should try out for handball. The handball coaches seemed to disagree as I never heard from them. Another friend got the call to try out for British cycling. Most of these flirtations with other sports go nowhere but they are a fun distraction from the big question, what am I going to do with the rest of my life?

A smattering of the retiring Olympians have entered the national consciousness, either through winning several gold medals at the same Olympics (Chris Hoy, Michael Phelps and Kelly Holmes), winning gold medals at sequential Olympics (Steve Redgrave), doing something truly amazing while being charismatic (Usain Bolt), doing something embarrassingly badly while being charismatic (Eddie the Eagle Edwards, Eric the Eel), being caught for drugs (Ben Johnson) or just being cute (Tom Daley). Each Olympics seems to create two or three national stars, just a handful of household names. There isn't room in the public eye or in the collective memory for more. Having a shorter, more memorable name probably helps fix a personality in the celebrity firmament and ideally one that makes for easy headline writing (after Chris Hoy's gold medal in the Athens kilometre cycle the following headlines made the press – 'Golden Boy Hoy; Golden Hoy; Hoy Wonder; Real McHoy').

Putting aside those who've remained in the public consciousness due to misdemeanours with drugs, the trickle of Olympic megastars have myriad options in the immediate aftermath of their Olympics. The most sought after, the holiest of holies of Olympic retirement, is a spot on the BBC sports commentary team, which is traditionally combined with sports writing for broadsheet newspapers. Only a very select few will get the call up, the vast majority of them gold medallists (surely it's time for a non-gold medallist loser to join the ranks? Someone who knows what it's like to strive, but to fail? Not to achieve their dream? To offer another perspective? My hand is up!).

The after dinner speech and corporate entertainment circuit can be lucrative and agents like London-based JLA have sprung up in the last couple of decades to help Olympians source and negotiate opportunities. It's particularly hard for newly anointed Olympians to suddenly realise they're a valuable commodity and, left to negotiate directly, most will vastly undersell themselves. Could you say with a straight face, I want £5,000 please for an hour of me talking about myself, plus expenses? The laws of supply and demand work just as surely on the value of Olympians as they do on oil, dollars or bails of wheat – the rarer the commodity, the higher the price. After Beijing, an Olympian like Tim Brabants with a single gold could command around £2.5k to £5k for a corporate speech. What's rarer than an Olympic gold medallist? A two-time Olympic gold medallist. James Cracknell, with gold in Athens and Sydney is in the next bracket. Moving up, to even greater rarity value, Sir Chris Hoy and Sir Matthew Pinsent with four golds each can command between £10k and £25k a speech.

Olympic coaches are also understandably in demand on the conference circuit. David Brailsford, performance director for British Cycling and widely reputed architect of the cycling team's success, can charge between £5k and £10k per event. Sir Clive Woodward, who guided England to rugby World Cup victory in 2003 and is now director of Elite Performance at the British Olympic Association, is in the £10k–£25k bracket.

These corporate speaking slots might sound like easy gigs but just because you're good at swimming or cycling or running doesn't mean you can speak well publicly in front of hundreds of bored executives.

Olympians can generally deal with pressure and adrenaline, and are confident in their own sphere of competence, but for most public speaking is well outside their comfort zone so they go through a quick learning process.

As '88 hockey gold medallist Steve Batchelor reminisced, 'They're not the easiest things to do. I've done schools, where I don't mind talking in front of 700 kids about the Olympics, but I do find corporate stuff hard work. You feel a lot of pressure so you want to make it good. I was advised to use prompt cards with bullet points to help.'

Steve's face turns grave with recollection, 'I was booked to do a 20-minute talk up at Beechams in Harlow. They had a massive great lecture theatre. These girls put mikes on me when I arrived and they were like, "We've had Tessa Sanderson and Ranulph Fiennes here." I was thinking, "Oh, shit."

'I stood up in front of about 150 people, got these cards out and I started my talk. I was going through the cards and I just completely lost my way and I stopped.' Anyone who's stuttered and stopped in a public speech can empathise. The initial blank shock that you've come to a halt mid-speech. The fear that builds with every passing second of silence. Your heart thumping like an express train, so loud you can't think. The silence lengthens and lengthens and feels more gigantic and more impossible to breach every second. And everyone is staring at you.

Steve continues, 'I felt like walking out and going home.' After a few more moments he resolved to give it another try. 'I apologised and told them I'm going to give the cards a miss and just talk to you about my experiences. And I did and they loved it. I've never used cards since. I got £700 for 20 minutes in 1989 [equivalent to almost £1,500 today]. A teammate used to get £4,000 to £5,000 for stuff he did. Then that was quite a lot. It is good money but you've got to be good or they won't ask you back and your agent won't book you for the next one.'

And it's not just speeches that provide opportunities for Olympians to monetise their success; product endorsements and grand openings of new offices or supermarkets are also common. Steve looks a little sheepish at the recollection of a product endorsement he did, 'Sean [Curley] and I sat on the bonnet of a new Ford. With a big breasted woman between us. She had a T-shirt on at the time, thank goodness. We got £500 each.'

Many gold medallists (and some silver and bronze medallists) take six months off after the Games to take maximum advantage of the peak in their public profile and squeeze in as many endorsements, appearances and speaking opportunities as possible. They have to take advantage of the publicity window. Unless you're a five time gold medallist your commercial value drops rapidly about six months after the Games and falls away again when the next Olympic Games comes around. The commercial opportunities are lucrative enough to attract scam artists trying to con Olympians out of their hard won earnings. Beijing 400m runner Andrew Steele, along with more than 20 track and field athletes, apparently fell victim to a fraudster who promised various sponsorship deals if he first paid £500 to get on the agency's books. Nothing ever materialised.

Another increasingly popular route for retired Olympians is executive coaching, business consulting and team building, the irony being that most pro-athletes have no experience of business whatsoever. Olympians have, however, worked with great coaches, understand how to deal with pressure and know what it's like to work in a well-motivated high performance team. As an Olympian you don't realise how rare these teams are until you quit being an athlete and enter the real world. Years following the Olympics, a CEO I work with introduced a test of employee engagement into his organisation called the Gallup Q^{12}. Engaged and motivated employees are more productive and passionate than clock watching and bored jobsworths, unsurprisingly. Out of curiosity I ran the test over a few of my Olympic squadmates. Average organisations score around 2:1 (denoting a 2:1 ratio of engaged employees to actively disengaged employees). Happily for the British team they scored in excess of 10:1, a 'world class' score (fortunate given they compete on the world stage). A really great team is a rare thing – a team (in the context of Olympians regardless of whether it is a support team working with a single athlete or a team of athletes) focussed ruthlessly on a clear joint goal. This is pure meritocracy, where each member takes responsibility for their own performance and are willing to sacrifice almost anything to achieve the team's goal.

Endorsements, journalism, public speaking and corporate coaching provide great opportunities for the handful of Olympic stars created by each Olympics. These few stars remain renowned and defined by their sporting greatness after retirement. For the majority of retiring Olympians however, those not on the front of cereal boxes, who have a couple of weeks as a minor celebrity before returning to anonymity, have to re-invent themselves in a whole new world. One in which many struggle to fit.

Lost

Returning to Earth after the Games frenzy settles down is tough. In the run up to the Olympics you can see nothing beyond the Games itself. All of your life and intensity is focused on that goal. Suddenly the Olympics arrives. Within two weeks it's over. After three months the post-Olympic celebrations have concluded. Your treasured and hard won Olympic kit is put away, neatly folded in the attic (when can you wear it out without looking like an idiot?). Then what?

As one veteran of three Olympics recalled, 'There's a big downer after the Olympics. You've been in the best place ever and then it's back to normality. It's like the end of a great holiday.'

Unfortunately, it gets far worse than just post-holiday blues. Time spits you out into uncharted territory, on the dark side of the moon which you've been unable to see until you're actually there. Everything suddenly seems utterly pointless. Looking back on the time when you were an athlete, the Olympics and all that, it feels like a different life that someone else lived. An Aussie medallist I spoke to agreed, 'On the odd occasion I'll get the medal out for a speaking engagement and I'll look at it and wonder – did that really happen? It's like a recurring dream.'

It was comforting to find in talking to others that I wasn't the only one that found it hard to adjust to normal, civilian life. British rower Josh West, veteran of Athens and Beijing echoed my experience.

'The celebratory mood [after the Olympics] falls away after a couple of months. The London parade was a good finale but by the end of the year the buzz was definitely gone. I still really miss sport. I find it really hard. The whole lifestyle of it, the fact you can focus on yourself and your performance and the physical pleasure you get out of it. The satisfaction and sense of immediate goals. The excitement of the whole thing. The fact there's a team and camaraderie around it. There's just so many things that make the adjustment almost impossible. For me it's been three years and I really honestly feel like I haven't completely adjusted.'

An American Olympian from Los Angeles had similar feelings. 'You've got all this excess energy because you're not training and you're high as a kite because you've been to the Olympics – it's a great drug. You're quite convinced you can do anything. But of course you can't. I mean you think everything is possible – you can move mountains or make millions of dollars or write a book. Unfortunately success in the sporting world doesn't necessarily help you unless you want to coach.'

Some like fencer Nick Bell throw themselves back into previous careers. 'I was very lucky because it wasn't the end of my world [after the Olympics]. It was just a suspended reality. After '76 I was back into doing 80 to 90 hour weeks in medicine so I didn't have time to feel sorry for myself. There were a few who went off the rails a bit, drank a bit. There wasn't the infrastructure to look after people afterwards. I do feel for current athletes, who put all their life into it. I wouldn't want to do that. It's not good for the psyche. It makes you have a skewed view of life. If you have a bad day of fencing it feels like your world's over.' And when you stop fencing entirely, what's left? Nothing.

Here's a Beijing medallist, 'Stopping after Beijing was interesting because it was tough. With London I could have easily persuaded myself to keep going but I decided that I wanted to do something different and make sure that I wasn't just doing sport because by that stage it's the easy thing to carry on doing. Stepping away from that is hard because that's all you know. And you're known as Bob the athlete and suddenly you're going, "Hang on a minute, I'm no longer Bob the athlete. What am I or who am I? What am I going to do, what's the rest of my life?" I don't think I'll ever get used to a desk. It amazes me that people do that for like 40 years of their lives. Do you not need fresh air and sun, guys? I have to ride my bike in and out. Like five times I've taken the train in two years – it's miserable.'

As the Beijing medallist highlights, it's not just the challenge of finding and starting a whole new career. Retiring after a Games many athletes don't just lose their jobs, they lose their whole identity, their sense of purpose and self-worth. Athletes build their entire identities around their sport. I'm an elite sportsman, therefore I am. Suddenly you're not an athlete anymore. You are nothing. This loss of self is emphasised by some Olympians struggling to fit back into the real world. A little like retired soldiers returned to civvy street, they've been away for years doing something of which they are immensely proud, which is full of adrenaline and camaraderie, and then it's time to start normality.

Normality is something into which they don't quite fit, the obvious exception being retired Olympic sailors who can do pretty well. With the America's Cup and corporate hospitality events, the sport is one where total novices can share Olympians' expertise as passengers on a yacht helmed by them. But apart from the sailors, modern Olympians without much (or sometimes any) prior work experience can struggle.

Some start on graduate training schemes in their mid-30s, alongside gaggles of 20-year-olds, and report to managers many years their junior. Their employers parade the ex-athletes around like a corporate bauble or prize bull, their first-hand experience of the Olympics making great talking points with clients and suppliers. Other retirees follow a natural path into coaching. Some just don't get jobs.

The social lives of Olympians change immensely on retirement. No longer the hours every day with teammates of a similar age and outlook, whom you know intimately from the months on training camp being able to look into each other's souls as you go through the furnace of the training programme.

Retired Olympians have to adapt physically as well. Olympians are used to heavy daily doses of endorphins, the body's natural pain-killers which are released during and after exercise and produce the so-called 'runners' high' sense of contentment. Similar hormones are released after sex or after eating chocolate. Olympians are also used to regular shots of adrenaline from racing and competitive training, which gives you a sensation of being totally alive and 'in the moment'. Some get over these addictions by going totally cold turkey and making up for it with hits of chocolate or other substances.

Most give into their cravings (and their vanity) and gradually wean themselves off, hitting the gym at lunchtime or running round the park after work or, in the case of triathlete Sian Brice, swimming at 5am each morning before work (even while pregnant). Some Olympians eventually discover that their craving for sport has damaged their longer term health and most have a long-term injury of some sort, a calling card to remind them of their other life. Runners suffer with their knees, and the regular friction on the kneecap can also cause lasting structural damage in tennis players, cyclists and football players. Rowers suffer lower back and disc problems (at the extreme requiring operations to remove spinal discs and fuse together vertebrae). It's rare to find a veteran of throwing sports, like javelin, without a dodgy shoulder or rotator cuff. Apart from mechanical problems, some develop thyroid problems (the gland that regulates the body's metabolism) in their early 30s, typically more common in post-menopausal women. Heart irregularities are also surprisingly common. Having developed huge, powerful hearts, when retirement comes the huge pump can fall into disrepair and start misfiring, producing all sorts of irregular heartbeat issues. Most of the athletes don't suffer any serious side effects but they are disturbing nonetheless. On the upside though, Olympians seem to have a lower incidence of heart disease.

Imagine changing your friends, job, self-image and moving house all at once. The drastic changes to social life, employment and the withdrawal of adrenaline and endorphins inevitably lead to problems. A minority can't control their eating and pile on weight, which doesn't help their confused self-image. One can't help making the unfortunate parallel between a fat, directionless ex-athlete and a depressed legacy city, of which there can be no better example than Athens. It's been reported (though disputed by Greek authorities) that the Olympic Village housing is only half full and 21 of the 22 venues lie closed and covered in graffiti, with anything of value, like copper piping, long since looted.

Apart from overeating, other Olympians find solace in drink, as Nick Bell mentioned. Some find drugs. I've seen previous Olympians out of their minds on cocaine several times (once, a couple of them, a Brit and a European, romped merrily through a bag of the stuff, interspersed with drags of weed).

Russell Garcia, who was alongside Steve Batchelor in the British hockey team in Seoul '88 and was the youngest hockey player ever to win an Olympic gold (aged only 18), built an illustrious career and became the most capped England player of all time with more than 300 appearances. But nothing could quite live up to that gold medal. In December 1999 at the age of 29 he failed a drugs test for cocaine. Thankfully Steve confirmed, 'That was a blip. He's fine again now.'

The post-Olympic transition is made harder by most Olympians not wanting to admit to their old teammates that they are struggling with the change. They're used to winning, to being amongst the best. They don't do perceived admissions of failure, so the retiring Olympians tend to face the transition alone. I spoke to British sports psychologist Chris Shambrook to better help me understand the post-Olympic come-down, which he's seen many times.

'With the energy that gets invested in an Olympics and how much of your heart and soul you pour into it, when it's over there is a big, big come-down; a gaping hole. You've just built up to the biggest moment of your career. Then your purpose goes. Your motivation goes. There is that sense that you've worked towards something and now actually the reason for doing it doesn't exist.

'We try and prepare people for it but those are difficult conversations to have with Olympians before the Games. You try and talk to them about it, "We really need to talk about how you're going to feel when the Olympics is over." They say, "Why? Don't distract me, I haven't qualified for it yet, I don't want to hear about it."

'Groups of sports psychologists get together and discuss the importance of preparing people for the come-down and the post Olympic depression and there should be stuff in place for that very predictable come-down. But of course it's after the performance. Who's going to pay for it? And anyway everyone goes on holiday.'

When they come back from holiday the retiring athletes return to a disconcerting emptiness, like they left part of themselves in the Olympic Village. Their old mentors, the coaches, have already moved on and have started plotting their next Olympic campaign (Shambrook has sat with a chief coach the day after the Olympic finals who was already plotting what the gold medal standard would be for the next Olympics). For the coaches the cycle goes on. For the retired athletes the wheels can just come off entirely.

I'd defined myself by my sport. My training sessions. My standing within the squad. My results. My Olympic goal. I was an athlete pure and simple. Then all of a sudden, I was nothing. I'd lost myself. The IOC defines it as 'identity foreclosure', not that I knew that at the time. My self-esteem went bust.

Shambrook nods as I recount my experience. 'There is a whole area of research around a concept called Athletic Identity. Athletic Identity is all about how closely my identity is allied to my performances as an athlete. If I am my results. If I am my performance. If I've handed "me" over to that – that puts me in a very, very challenging place when the results and the performances aren't there anymore. And it's doubly challenging because you have to get pretty close to handing your personality over to that [mentality] in order to give yourself the best chance of winning. But it leaves you very vulnerable afterwards.'

In other words, in order to win you have to lose all perspective. Everything else must fall away. You have to become your performances. You are either a good or a bad person, a success or a failure depending on the time on the stopwatch. On the edge of madness, if not over the edge.

Shambrook agrees, 'There is a fine line between the mental health practitioner's perspective and an elite coach's and athlete's perspective, to be honest. As a psychologist in the world of elite sport the mental health of people isn't always the primary concern.'

I hadn't even recognised I had an 'Athletic Identity'. Like most people I hadn't given any thought to how I define myself or what drove or undermined my self-esteem, but it was comforting to discover that the phenomenon was recognised and that many others had gone through it. All the Olympians I spoke to had suffered the adjustment pains to varying degrees but the more recent Olympians, who are able to train full time thanks to the funding schemes available in countries like the US, Australia and the UK, they get hit worst, no doubt because their professionalism allows a stronger Athletic Identity to be created and then destroyed when they retire.

Even the gold medallists struggle with it. One I know well was diagnosed with depression within a year or so of sporting retirement.

A period on medication followed and he continued with therapy for years. Another, an American gold medallist, talks about having 'survivor's guilt' which took her a long time to get over. On hearing that another Olympian quipped, 'Survivor's guilt compares favourably with loser's guilt, I can promise you that.'

After Chris Shambrook introduced me to the concept of Athletic Identity, I discovered that the IOC publishes a leaflet on it and managing the transition from sport. The IOC notes that, for top athletes, 'Athletic Identity is central as they dedicate 100 per cent of time and resources to pursuit of sporting goals.'

To prevent the collapse of the self the IOC calls 'identity foreclosure', they recommend athletes have other interests (whether professional, social or just other hobbies) to reduce 'exclusive identification with the sporting self' and that athletes should prepare adequately for a career outside sport, instead of waiting for the sports career to end before being forced to take the leap. I can't agree with this strongly enough. When in training for the Olympics it's all too easy to go home exhausted, stick on the TV and stay in your athletic comfort zone. Olympians – take my advice. Plan ahead. One day either you'll quit your sport or it will quit you. When that happens, be ready for the next chapter in your life. There are other things in life to achieve and to enjoy.

The IOC note on transitioning from sport also recommends the development of 'solid stress management and time management skills'. These steps will 'help minimise the shock experienced at the moment you retire from sport'. I've never met a top level athlete without those capabilities. It's these characteristics and others that allow many Olympians, after a period of transition, to turn what got them to the Olympics into a driving force for success in the Olympic after-life.

Redirecting the rocket

What gets an athlete to the Olympics can take them onto other great things. Getting to the Olympics obviously requires self-control, maturity (just look at Tom Daley) and a capacity for lots of hard work. When you're an elite sportsperson, even in the evening after a hard day's training or during a day off you're never really off the clock. You're just refuelling, resting and getting enough sleep for maximum muscle recovery. Not that we had many days off. I had nine days without training in the 365 days running up to Athens. As my coach used to remind us, your body doesn't know it's a weekend or bank holiday. For a few months after starting work I remember being pleasantly surprised at weekends when they rolled around. Suddenly I had oodles of time and was able to do just what I wanted, not that I knew what I wanted to do. The effect wore off soon enough and now I take the glory of weekends for granted like everyone else.

Some Olympians make the transition successfully, applying the intensity and focus from the Games into 'real life'. Here's one gold medallist:

'I think you always use it, I think it's just the nature of who you are. You look for mentors within the working environment, someone who's been over the potholes before you. Workwise I think you naturally put in short and long-term goals which you aspire to do.'

Here's another gold medallist, an American this time, ruminating on life after the Olympics, 'You learn discipline, of course, and that's useful in every aspect of life – you couldn't be the best drug dealer in the world or whatever without discipline. The Olympics and training for it is good at training that muscle in your psyche. In retrospect, I should have used that discipline to make some money. Everyone knows the saying that on your death bed you're not going to say "I wish I'd spent more time in the office". But I'm the guy who probably should have spent more time in the office.'

Olympian Adrian Moorhouse at the other extreme has spent a lot of time in many different offices. Adrian co-founded performance development consultancy Lane4 with sports psychologist Professor Graham Jones in 1995, seven years after swimming to gold in Seoul '88 (Lane4 being Moorhouse's lane for the Olympic final), to bring the magic dust of Olympic greatness to business. It seems to have worked. Lane4 has grown rapidly and now boasts clients like Coca-Cola, Honda and Sainsbury's. It seems no organisation is too big not to want a sprinkling of Olympian performance.

Across the pond, surely one of the recent most financially successful Olympians is Porter Collins, an American who rowed to fifth place in the men's eight in Atlanta and Sydney. After retiring from rowing he moved into finance in New York, with stints at Chilton Investment Company and Goldman Sachs, before moving with Steve Eisman to start hedge fund FrontPoint. As recalled in the popular book *The Big Short* by Michael Lewis, Eisman and Collins saw the madness of the US subprime property market before the bubble burst and bet heavily against it, reputedly making their investors billions and themselves millionaires many times over in the process.

Another Olympian friend of mine, who won gold in 2000 and carried on in the sport for another eight years without ever quite capturing his Sydney form, eventually joined pre-eminent management consultancy McKinsey and Co. McKinsey has an imposing reputation as the best known strategy consulting firm in the world. Top executives at multi-national companies go to McKinsey, discreetly, when they have a problem which needs solving. McKinsey take no prisoners, don't suffer fools (I should know, they rejected my application), and practise an 'up-or-out' policy – you either progress or you get fired. My friend says his previous head coach ran the same system, and that the team dynamic, intensity and performance atmosphere remind him of his Olympic days. Several other Olympians I know have made careers in the City, working across banking, private equity, trading, venture capital and law. Researching this book I stumbled upon an Olympian lawyer whom I didn't know, a family law barrister called Joanna Toch. A veteran of both Moscow and the Los Angeles Olympics, Toch's mission statement as stated on her website is clear of the benefits of her sporting experience in her work today:

> In my sporting career I learned to be successful by personal commitment, thorough preparation, teamwork, being calm under pressure, fearlessness and self-belief ... I believe every one of these qualities is essential to my work at the family Bar in every case I undertake.

Outside of the City, Olympians can be found successfully operating in numerous niches, in teaching, the military, sports coaching, the family business, even Formula One teams. Tom Stallard, who took silver with Josh West in the British men's eight in Beijing, joined the McLaren Formula One team just a few weeks after the Olympics. No doubt his experience of the high performing British rowing team helps him in the fast-paced team environment of Formula One. Today he's Jensen Button's performance engineer and travels the world with the Formula One circus. Unknowingly he took the IOC's advice on preparing for transition and his hobbies during his Olympics training prepared him well for his new career. In 2003 he bought an AC Cobra car kit as a project to keep him busy when not training in the run up to Athens. He finally finished it in 2008 after his Beijing medal, only to have the Cobra's engine blow up the second time out. Hopefully Tom can tune Jensen's front wing more reliably and take less than five years.

Whether driving in Formula One or pistol shooting at the Olympics, athletes tend to have addictive and obsessive personalities. On retirement these traits can either be a force for bad (drink, drugs or depression) or a force for good, if they can be channelled in the right direction, allowing the ex-athlete's maniacal focus and drive to take them into a successful new chapter of their lives.

Geoff Capes putted the shot for Great Britain at the Munich, Montreal and Moscow Olympics (and at 64 other international competitions). He went on to be twice crowned the World's Strongest Man, in 1983 and 1985. Today his obsession has swung a very different direction: breeding prize budgerigars, specifically Recessive Pieds. Geoff links his athletic success with his prize winning birds, saying, 'With my budgerigars, as in my sport, I will always strive for perfection.' Geoff was elected President of the Budgerigar Society's General Council in 2009.

Fencer Nick Bell also recognises an obsessional personality trait in himself. 'I am driven. If I want something I can really focus on it, possibly to the detriment of other things. Talking earlier about the winners not being very nice people, unless one's careful, one can be too self-absorbed to the detriment of those immediately round you. You have to reflect on that. Maybe I was a bit obsessed.'

Today Nick, the eccentric and gangly doctor, who now has rather more sensible hair than in his Olympic days (black 1980s McEnroe beehive), obsesses about things other than fencing. When I visit his home near Oxford a black antique-looking car radiator covers the kitchen table and betrays his new hobby, collecting and restoring vintage cars.

After we've talked about his Olympics he proudly shows me the collection. Four or five of the gleaming machines fill his drive but the real classics are kept in his large garage, which is strewn with car parts and tools.

'That's a 1919 Sizaire-Berwick, very rare,' he says smiling at a big grey wedding car. 'Brought it over from New Zealand. The next one's a 1928 Ford Model A.' Next to that is a bright yellow vintage car which looks like the vehicle of choice of Toad from *The Wind in the Willows*.

Nick sees me looking at it. 'That's a 1927 Vauxhall 30-98. It was the first proper sports car built. A 100 mph machine. Haven't quite got it all the way there,' he says eyeing it hungrily. Clearly 100mph is on the to-do list. I'd be terrified at 20mph in the antique.

'Ebay is a great thing,' Nick nods. 'You've heard of premature e-clickulation? I'm constantly buying parts from America and importing them. It requires an awful lot of obsessive follow up and commitment. To find all the parts, put them together and get them running. Having done all that training, after no sleep, or if it's raining or it's cold, you're prepared to put the extra bit in, I think.'

Vintage cars give Nick something other than fencing to obsess about but I wonder how he replaces the excitement of competition and the endorphin rush.

'Absolutely. I still fence now. I'm a bit of a legend actually,' he can't help a smile. 'If you really want to know, I've been very lucky. I'm left handed and tall and have a very unorthodox style. I spent 33 years doing foil fencing but as I was doing less training the youngsters started beating me. I thought sod this I'm going to do epee, which is a much more cautious game. So in 1997 I stopped foil fencing and I went over to epee. Within two years I was ranked second in the country and made the British team. I went to the 1999 World Championships in South Korea. I was the oldest person there aged 49. I didn't do very well, I was out in the second round, but I was out there.

'So that was quite fun.' For a moment I think that's the end of story, the glorious last comeback, but I'm mistaken. 'I did epee until 2004 and in that time foil fencing evolved. The blades got whippier and more flexible which allowed you to make flick hits. The whole technique changed and the governing body changed the rules, which suited my type of fencing. So I went back to foil, to a whole new generation of fencers who didn't know who this 54-year-old was. My second competition [in foil] was the Welsh Open in November '04. The British fencer who'd gone to the Sydney Games and came 10th was there. But I won it! And I never even won that competition when I was a fit youngster. It caused quite a stir in the fencing world. Everyone was twittering about it.' Certainly more so than after Nick's 1976 Olympics, it's safe to bet.

Most other Olympians keep involved in their sport to some degree after retirement; it's difficult to give something up entirely when it has brought you so much success. Sian Brice for example, now a mother of two, had just ridden the Etape du Tour event the weekend before we met. The Etape is a race over a stage of the Tour de France, put on each year for enthusiastic (and mad) amateur riders. Sian's Etape stage took in the famous 21 hairpins of the Alpe D'Huez in 40 degree heat. She's thinking about entering the six day long Marathon des Sables next year, a 250km ultra-marathon. Rather self-depreciating, she closes, 'I guess I have always maintained a fitness level. I just needed less buzzes as time went on.'

Sian gets her regular training dose at her swimming club, the StAM (St Albans Masters). Her enthusiasm is enchanting, 'I love it. Masters swimming is amazing. There are all sorts in the pool – barristers, IT people, women who run their own companies, mums, but you're all in your swimming trunks and hat, and no one knows or cares what you do until you chat later. We just have a laugh, take the piss out of each other and train as hard as we can. Some of the guys are world record holders for their age in the 50m breast stroke, even though a few have really big pot bellies.' Each week Sian swims for an hour and a half on a Thursday night and an hour Sunday night after she's got the kids in bed and cooked her husband his tea. She is super-mum.

Family becomes the natural focus for many female Olympians, like Sian. Susie Murphy turned her attention to raising her two boys after her three Olympics. The Aussie gold medallist is similarly focused on bringing up her kids, which is particularly tough as her son is autistic. She is putting her Olympic determination to particularly good use.

'I always felt like an Olympic gold medal was like reaching for the stars. It's a goal you work towards. Now I feel like I'm doing the same with autism. Can I get on top of autism and epilepsy? It's the greatest challenge I've ever faced, getting my child back from severe disability. It far exceeds any stress I've ever been through [with the Olympics]. Any time a seizure happens I feel like I'm injecting myself with pure adrenaline. I used to think I got nervous but it had nothing on this. I'm arming myself with knowledge and leaving no stone unturned trying to help my son. It's frustrating, it's time consuming but I'm very determined and won't give up hope. Going for the Olympic gold medal was unrealistic but that was attainable.'

Others mentor younger sportspeople, like Steve Batchelor with his hockey and tennis academy. Bas van de Goor has found his new calling working to improve the quality of life of his fellow diabetes sufferers through his foundation, which promotes sport for those with the disease. The Australian gold medallist I interviewed was an Athlete Liaison Officer (ALO) with the Australian support team in Beijing. She was reluctant to talk to a Brit about it but the Australians take out previously winning athletes to mentor and coach the next crop.

'Yeah, I mentored in Beijing. I can't bring myself to talk about the mentoring stuff. I'm not British and it's hard to talk to the other side! In Beijing mentoring we'd be up at 6am going through to midnight. I was mentoring 10 or 12 sports a day. You remember the IOC pass you always wanted, infinite access? I had one. I went to all the sports. It was magic. I felt like God. I did quite a bit of mentoring with Steve Waugh. We'd go and meet athletes after training. Fencing in the morning, basketball in the evening, synchronised swimming, all sorts. It's not about the technicalities of all the sports, the athletes know that better than us, but the principles for mentoring are pretty universal. There's a top 10 which I always go through. But that top 10 I keep very much to Australia.'

The same Australian athlete also worked for the UN thanks to her Olympic heritage.

'I was a Goodwill Ambassador for four years. I never got to meet Angelina Jolie, that's the first thing everyone asks. When you talk about the Olympics allowing you to meet famous people, for me the most memorable meetings were with the kids in the refugee camps on the Thai/Cambodian border where the Khmer Rouge had been. We were filming for a documentary in these fields of landmines. The gold medal got a fair knocking about with all these kids handing it round. One kid dropped it so there's a big dent in it.'

So Olympians end up in all sorts of bizarre pursuits from tramping in minefields to brick laying to Formula One teams. I suppose I turned to writing. Even with their new fields, most find they can never leave their sport entirely and end up coaching or they just keep competing.

Triple Olympian Susie Murphy recently joined her local fencing club after decades out of the sport.

'One of my old fencing buddies, an old boyfriend actually, started a fencing club at the school round the corner. I've joined the beginners' class and it's fab. I love it. None of them know what I've done. I told the coach I don't want them to know. I'm Mrs Nobody. I had my first bout with a few younger guys the other day. They obviously thought, for a beginner she's not bad.'

If you're a member of a London fencing club and a middle-aged lady just demolished you, don't feel too bad. You may have fallen victim to another Secret Olympian.

Beijing
18 August 2008

Stepping out of the shiny new airport I take my first lungful of non air-conditioned Beijing. It's like drinking gritted smog soup despite the factory closures. In the bus we pass mile after mile of high rise grey offices, all shiny new. The Chinese economic miracle really is happening. Adorning the office frontages are billboards of the Olympic corporate sponsors, the usual sugary drinks, credit cards, fast food and IT providers, and Yao Ming the basketball player who is everywhere as the latest face of the Games linking East and West. Superficially it reminds me of Athens but having exchanged emails with an old teammate to get the lay of the land, I know that, whilst the circus of the Olympics is very similar, the backdrop is very different.

The food for starters. Duck tongues in jelly. Fried scorpions. Jellyfish. And this is in the touristy restaurants off Tiananmen Square. On the walk to the square tannoys proclaim 'maintain public order' and other civic reminders. The many China Central TV channels only show events in which Chinese athletes have won gold, interspersed with the occasional interview with African politicians who roundly endorse the 'Chinese model of democracy' over the 'colonial Western ideal'. At Olympic events there are official looking 'cheerers' in the stands, who hand out Chinese flags and red T-shirts with white Chinese script to anyone who'll have them (the T-shirts probably read 'this westerner's an idiot'). These pros then lead the crowd in chanting for the Chinese teams. At the boxing in the Workers Stadium the other night these professional supporters had the entire stadium whipped into a frenzy of cheering for the Chinese bantam-weight, all aside from my friend's small gaggle of Brits who rooted for the Moldovan underdog. Moldova (population 3 million) duly vanquished

China (population 1.3 billion). What felt like the entire stadium walked out, halfway through the night's competition. I hope my athlete buddies won't have to race in front of empty stands. That's not how you visualise the biggest moment of your life.

I've wondered for weeks how I'll feel watching my old teammates and the next generation of Olympians take on the world, writing the next chapters in their sporting obituaries whilst mine is long since concluded. While thousands here and back home scream for them, will I be in the stands, a nobody wracked by remorse at having quit? For years I've suffered repeated urges to walk away from my nascent new career and launch a comeback. Granted, the intervals between pangs of longing have increased as I've adjusted, but the thought has lingered there in the back of my mind, particularly in the warm summer months of the racing season.

I guess I have restarted my life. I moved on from my first job after three years to a much smaller firm where I don't have a ten digit personnel number and can actually make a difference. Some of the guys there are ex-athletes. Real team players. We're growing fast and it's exciting to be part of it. Sure, I still feel a quiet pride when I reverently put on my Olympic team cufflinks before work but then I get home and find my girlfriend towelling the cat dry with my Team GB towel. That keeps me grounded. I'm now getting into my weekend brunches in the sunshine with friends and family. I don't have that itch, the feeling I should be doing some else, something 'constructive'. And actually making it to weddings and birthday parties is pretty great, as is going on skiing holidays without being permanently worried about ruining an Olympic cycle with a broken leg. Sure, I'm still involved with my sport a little, a bit of coaching and some weekend training but nothing ungodly early and I choose my races based on exotic locations rather than international standing. In fact, now I'm in the country regularly enough we've got a dog. Next step, starting a family. I want all of that.

As the endless high rise office blocks flash by I realise that, the more I think about it, the more I'm struck by an absence of regret about retiring. I can't help but smile. Perhaps I am finally free of it. I feel for the box that holds the engagement ring in the top of my rucksack for the 100th time. I hope she says yes.

Before I take to one knee on a beach after Beijing, I get to cheer on my friends as they strive for greatness at the biggest sporting event in the world. What will this Olympics bring? Inevitably another chapter in the arms race between the dopers and the drug testers. And further escalation in the level of commercialisation and sponsorship. But the temple of excellence will also bring us new heroes. Proper heroes. Heroes that are genuinely great at something, not reality TV stars or frolicking young royals. For two weeks we can worship excellence not celebrity. We can cheer men and women that have sacrificed to be here, not Premiership footballers who won't get off the bench. We can worship victory and the striving for greatness and applaud those that may live the rest of their lives in the shadow of these two weeks.

For a few days both Olympians and fans can celebrate the greatness of their countries without embarrassment. We Brits can let ourselves feel national pride and banish that creeping feeling that we are gradually vanishing from the international stage. More importantly, for two weeks every four years the world has an excuse to come together and be united in celebration, rather than divided in dispute.

While I've come to realise there is more to life than endlessly pursuing a medal, I'm glad I had the experience. I know what goes on away from the cameras, outside the arena. Beforehand, the electric anticipation mixed with the tears and the madness, but also the forging of the deepest unbreakable friendships in the cauldron of pressure. Then the Village and its wonderful menagerie and celebration of human diversity. The incomparable sensation of being alive as you enter the arena for battle at the pinnacle of your career. The great parties. Afterwards, when we get home and the dust settles, I know I need to be there for my retiring comrades as they go through the invisible, lonely and jarring transition to a different life. But before all that we all get to celebrate the next instalment of heroism and human nature at the ultimate human race.

ACKNOWLEDGEMENTS

I'd like to sincerely thank all the Olympians with whom I spoke, both on and off the record, for giving their time and allowing a total stranger to pepper them with questions, some rather personal. So thanks to Tom James, BR, Steve Batchelor, KS, Sian Brice, EL, Nick Bell, BAL, Susie Murphy, G, Chris Shambrook and the team at K2 Performance Systems, Josh West, and Bas van de Goor, who through his foundation is doing great work for those with diabetes.

I wouldn't have been in a position to write this without having enjoyed both the support of my parents through all my sporting escapades and the insight of my coaches through the years, particularly PM, RB, DFL and RW. Thanks, KW, for being a great partner in crime throughout that summer, and to the whole squad for sharing the obsession.

Thanks to my family for their contributions and contacts and for supporting me in writing mode. My witches' coven of Nic, Jo and S provided invaluable thoughts and edits on late drafts.

David Luxton, at Luxton Harris, steered the idea down the right track and then into the right harbour. The whole team at Bloomsbury, including Naomi Webb, Ellen Williams and Emily Sweet, have been great. Huge thanks to Charlotte Atyeo in particular, who both spawned the genesis of this book with me, whilst listening to tall tales of the Olympics over a few gin and tonics, and had the patience to see beyond and develop the early drafts.

Lastly, thanks to all those Olympians past and present who've inspired with their passion and performance, medallists or not.